THIS IS ONLY A TEST

Teaching for Mathematical Understanding in an Age of Standardized Testing

NANCY LITTON & MARYANN WICKETT

D1275604

Math Solutions

SAUSALITO, CA

Math Solutions
150 Gate 5 Road
Sausalito, CA 94965
www.mathsolutions.com

The publisher would like to thank the following states, which gave permission to reprint borrowed material:

Arizona: Permission for use of material has been granted by the Arizona Department of Education.

California: Reprinted, by permission, California Department of Education, CDE Press, 1430 N Street, Suite 3207, Sacramento, CA 95814.

Florida: The Florida Comprehensive Assessment Test® (FCAT) Mathematics item appears by permission of the Florida Department of Education, Office of Assessment, Tallahassee, Florida 32399-0400.

Illinois: Copyright © 1997–2008, Illinois State Board of Education, reprinted by permission. All rights reserved.

Maryland: Permission for use of material has been granted by the Maryland State Department of Education.

New Mexico: Permission for use of material has been granted by the New Mexico State Department of Education.

Library of Congress Cataloging-in-Publication Data

Litton, Nancy, 1947–
    This is only a test : teaching for mathematical understanding in an age of standardized testing / Nancy Litton and Maryann Wickett.
        p. cm.
    Summary: "Guides teachers in planning instruction that takes standardized testing into account while staying focused on a curriculum that encourages students to love and understand mathematics"—Provided by publisher.
    ISBN 978-0-941355-87-2 (alk. paper)
    1. Mathematics—Study and teaching (Elementary)—United States. 2. Effective teaching—United States. 3. Achievement tests—United States. I. Wickett, Maryann. II. Title.
    QA135.6.L575 2009
    377.7'2—dc22

                                                                    2008024643

Editor: Toby Gordon
Production: Melissa L. Inglis-Elliott
Cover design: Jenny Jensen Greenleaf
Interior design: Joni Doherty Design
Composition: ICC Macmillan Inc.

Printed in the United States of America on acid-free paper
12 11 10 09 08   ML   1 2 3 4 5

A Message from Math Solutions

We at Math Solutions believe that teaching math well calls for increasing our understanding of the math we teach, seeking deeper insights into how children learn mathematics, and refining our lessons to best promote students' learning.

Math Solutions shares classroom-tested lessons and teaching expertise from our faculty of Math Solutions professional development instructors as well as from other respected math educators. Our publications are part of the nationwide effort we've made since 1984 that now includes

- more than five hundred face-to-face inservice programs each year for teachers and administrators in districts across the country;
- annually publishing professional development books, now totaling more than seventy titles and spanning the teaching of all math topics in kindergarten through grade 8;
- four series of videos for teachers, plus a video for parents, that show math lessons taught in actual classrooms;
- on-site visits to schools to help refine teaching strategies and assess student learning; and
- free online support, including grade-level lessons, book reviews, inservice information, and district feedback, all in our *Math Solutions Online Newsletter*.

For information about all of the products and services we have available, please visit our website at *www.mathsolutions.com*. You can also contact us to discuss math professional development needs by calling (800) 868-9092 or by sending an email to *info@mathsolutions.com*.

We're always eager for your feedback and interested in learning about your particular needs. We look forward to hearing from you.

Math Solutions®

Contents

Contents

Introduction

This book emerged from our belief that teachers have a primary responsibility to prepare students to be mathematical thinkers who are fully prepared to meet the challenges they will face in life, long after all the bubbles on the tests have been filled in. It was written for teachers who strive to help children develop mathematical understandings that make sense to them and will lay the foundation for long-term growth in mathematical thinking. It's designed for teachers who want to develop a balanced approach to assessment that leads to better teaching practices, practices that have the added benefit of being likely to result in higher standardized test scores.

We want teachers to move away from the notion that students need a steady diet of multiple-choice worksheets all year long in order to do well on standardized math tests. We even want to dispel the notion that as the test date approaches, it's appropriate to ask students to memorize incomprehensible procedures and algorithms that leave them feeling confused and unable to trust their own knowledge. We want to lessen the need for reteaching because students have forgotten poorly understood procedures and have little conceptual base on which to build new learning.

Most of us became teachers because of our strong hope of making a positive difference in our students' lives. Teachers like being with children and want to provide them with the very best opportunities for learning. So we search out best teaching practices, build on our own experiences of what is and is not effective, and often feel deeply gratified with our work. In our role as teachers, we make decisions that affect our students and spend countless hours reflecting on and refining our choices.

The process of making the best choices for our students is not always easy. Pressure to increase test scores can be overwhelming. The details might look different from district to district, depending on the socioeconomics of the student population. However, at both low- and high-performing schools the pressure is real and can lead to decisions about practices that prevent children from constructing mathematical understandings that will serve them well in testing and in life.

The underlying purpose of the current testing situation is to ensure that all children have the basic skills needed to be successful, productive citizens. We believe that good teaching supports strong learning and is ultimately the best preparation for testing. This text is designed to help combat the panic that teachers and administrators often succumb to—foregoing good instruction for short, quick fixes such as memorizing mathematics vocabulary out of context and teaching mathematical procedures with little or no understanding.

Good math teaching and success on tests can go hand in hand if teachers

- develop a learning environment that encourages children's natural curiosity and enthusiasm for learning,

- make careful decisions that help students build deep understanding of mathematical ideas,

- help students make connections among important mathematical ideas and apply their knowledge to new, unfamiliar situations, and

- encourage a belief within each student that he or she can understand the mathematics.

Instructional practices such as these build within students a strong knowledge base that stays with them and grows as they move from grade to grade. Students truly own and can use this understanding to succeed in future learning and on tests.

We know how ephemeral test results can be even if we manage to raise test scores. Scores tend to be low the first time students take a particular standardized test and then rise each subsequent year as we become more adept at preparing children for that test. When a new test is introduced, the scores may plummet. Students may have learned to take one particular test, but are not able to transfer their abilities to a new test.

It's important to acknowledge that there are also many influences on teaching and testing that are beyond the control of schools, teachers, and learners. Some influences are as simple and common as a spat with a friend on the playground, a poor night's sleep, or an insufficient breakfast. More serious issues affecting teaching and learning include, but are not limited to, the literacy level of parents, a primary home language other than English, poverty and the violence that may accompany it, an impending or recent divorce, single-parent challenges, parents who both work and don't have time to help with homework, parents who are unavailable and possibly in situations that cause anxiety to their families (on active military duty, in jail, etc.), and inadequate health care. Add these factors to the political pressure to raise test scores and it becomes easy to see why classroom teachers sometimes succumb to the desire for quick fixes.

This book offers a different path to consider. Developing a classroom culture that establishes trust and respect among students and teacher along with using good teaching practices that result in the deep understanding of mathematical concepts are the most effective ways to achieve success in all aspects of school, including testing.

Through this book, we offer you strategies that have helped our students feel confident and able to perform well on standardized tests without compromising our basic beliefs about how children learn. The suggestions for test preparation match our strongly held beliefs about good teaching practices that we use throughout the year. In addition, we have become well versed in our state standards and acquainted with the types of tests our students must take. This knowledge can then be applied to finding ways to help students link their understanding with the test. Giving thought to this important part of our students' learning experience provides us with the satisfaction that we've been responsible in an area that has significant consequences for them.

There's a positive aspect to this work. Although there are times we lament the idea that the standardized test writers seem to know far too little about what is age appropriate for young students, and this complaint is often legitimate, we can use the tests and their content to help us improve some aspects of our teaching. Simple computation is not the primary focus of standardized state math tests, nor is it enough to ensure students will do well in school and beyond. Today students are expected to understand and apply a wide variety of mathematical ideas, as delineated by state standards. The standards compel us to expand our vision of mathematics beyond arithmetic while ensuring that all of our students understand and apply important math concepts to solve problems. Our job is to cut through the convoluted language of the standards and the test, first for our own deeper understanding of the math, and then with our students, so that they have access to mathematical ideas that they will need in order to be successful in their studies and in life.

This book will provide you with ways to take control of the test-preparation process, rather than have it control you, your students, and your curriculum. Every standardized test is different, so no one can provide you with a simple blueprint for appropriate test preparation. But with some effort and ingenuity, and possibly some brainstorming with colleagues, you can create a plan that has the potential to assist your students and free you from some of the emotional drain that worrying about testing places on you as a caring professional.

I

Understanding Assessment

One of the biggest issues in mathematics education today is the tension between what we consider to be good teaching and the demands for raising scores on standardized tests. Teachers often feel caught between the desire to give students the time they need to develop understanding of mathematical ideas and the pressure for producing higher test scores. In this section, we explore the meaning of formative assessment and its role in standardized testing (summative assessment), address some of the issues surrounding standardized testing, and help teachers develop strategies for meeting both of these goals.

Chapter 1

Making Formative Assessment Count

Summative Assessment Versus Formative Assessment

Good teaching requires constant assessment on the part of the classroom teacher. When thinking about the kind of assessment that teachers need to use most often as they go about the business of helping students develop their mathematical abilities, it is helpful to make a distinction between two major types of assessments:

- *Summative assessment* is designed to measure what a student has learned at the end of a set of learning experiences. Tests given at the end of a teaching unit fall into this category, as do standardized tests. States and school districts use this type of assessment primarily to evaluate school programs.

- *Formative assessment,* on the other hand, has the goal of providing feedback that can be used to improve teaching and learning throughout the year, ultimately leading to students who are more prepared to take a standardized test later in the year. It's important to understand and value this type of assessment, according it at least as much importance as standardized testing, since it can serve the purpose of helping us improve instruction on a day-to-day basis, all year long.

The summative assessment addressed in this book is standardized testing. The next few pages explore how formative assessment can play a significant role in preparing for summative assessment.

A Closer Look at Formative Assessment

Formative assessment involves observing students, listening to them, and examining the work they produce. It allows a teacher to understand in some detail what students do and don't know and helps with effective day-to-day planning. Formative assessment can take the form of carefully attending when students are asked to share ideas with one another in small- and large-group settings. Such discussions give children invaluable practice validating and supporting conjectures with mathematical arguments. These discussions also provide useful assessment opportunities to the teacher who listens intently and respectfully to students, taking note of how they are thinking and reasoning.

Equally important are the many conversations that take place as a teacher circulates through the classroom, chatting with individuals about how they're going about solving a problem. These conversations are designed primarily for the purpose of supporting students in their learning and often include asking questions that cause a child to think in new ways or to provide more in-depth answers to problems. By noting how a student responds to these nudges, teachers can also use these informal chats to learn how the child is thinking and reasoning.

The written work that students produce in response to a problem is another form of formative assessment. Asking students to solve open-ended tasks that can be approached in more than one way offers access to all students and encourages them to reason, make connections, and communicate about mathematics. The work that gets produced in response to this kind of assignment gives teachers concrete evidence to carefully reflect on when the school day is over. Written work can help teachers understand the level of mathematical reasoning, flexibility, and efficiency of each child, illustrating how the child solves problems and revealing his ability to organize and communicate thinking in written form. This written work can form the basis of conversations with the whole class to convey new and useful strategies for other students to consider and can also be used in individual conferences with students. These individual follow-up conferences have the potential to move a student to new levels of understanding as teacher and student discuss the work, finding ways to move beyond misconceptions or incomplete understandings.

Individual conferences based on more formal assessments, ones that are specifically devised to probe for understanding about a particular concept, are also useful. For instance, a formal place-value assessment given early in second grade can provide information about each child's present level of understanding. Third-grade teachers may want to look closely at each child's operational understanding of multiplication. Teachers at each grade level want to know where students are as they begin or progress through the year or a unit of study.

Lainie Schuster reminds us that "as teachers, we are diagnosticians of student growth and achievement" (2009, 56). She confirms that formative assessments can help us gain important knowledge about these areas:

- the strengths, weaknesses, and needs of each new class and each student

- students' fluency with basic facts

- students' ability to apply operational understandings to problem-solving situations

- how students apply number sense to their calculation strategies

- the factors that dictate students' choice of strategies

- how likely students are to apply the same strategy over and over, versus use the numbers and/or context of problems to determine the procedures they use

- how well and with what methods students are able to articulate their understandings

Schuster's ultimate goal is one that we all share—to figure out how our students *know* and *do* mathematics so that we can help them grow.

Keeping track of formative assessment

Some teachers have the ability to hold much of this type of assessment in their heads, using their students' written work to help them maintain an accurate picture of how the students are progressing. Others prefer to keep written records. Schuster (2009) suggests setting up a spiral-bound notebook with a separate section for each child. She realistically acknowledges that she has time to keep only cryptic notes; she dates each of her entries and during the first month of the school year comments on

- number sense
- fact fluency
- application of appropriate and efficient strategies
- reasoning ability
- ability and willingness to self-correct
- enthusiasm level

- interpersonal skills
- frustration levels

Schuster tries to comment on the same skills for every child so that she can take the pulse of both individual students and the class as a whole. She also finds it important to make personal connections with each student as she is collecting data. Ultimately all of the data, and her reflection on them, prove to be extremely useful in guiding her as she devises ongoing plans to help her students develop mathematically over the course of the school year.

Using formative assessments for classroom and district planning

It's interesting to note that with ample formative assessments, summative assessments become less important for classroom purposes. Teachers who do lots of formative assessments know where their students are and can devote more time to teaching and less time to testing.

Formative assessments sometimes reveal that students have understandings and strategies that show greater mathematical prowess than the teacher expected. At other times they might unmask a lack of understanding. With the knowledge gained through the many forms of formative assessments that take place on almost a daily basis, a teacher can provide a program based on an intimate knowledge of current student understanding. Such a program is likely to be much more effective than one that is focused primarily on ritualized practice for the standardized test.

Often school districts, in their attempt to make sure that students are ready to perform well on the standardized tests, decide to add still more summative assessments during the year. The result is that there is less time for teaching and also a rigid schedule that doesn't take into account the pace at which children acquire skills and construct knowledge. Teachers who have greater knowledge about the importance of formative assessments and how they will use these assessments throughout the year to effectively prepare their students have a better chance of working successfully with their local administrators and school boards. Chapter 9, "Communicating with Administrators and Parents," provides some suggestions for interacting effectively with district officials.

Teaching for Understanding

We want to acknowledge that teaching for understanding, including tuning in to student learning, is a difficult task full of hard decisions. When learning about how a child is currently performing, we must try to remember that students need time to interact with ideas, tools with which to build models, and opportunities to make mistakes on their way to becoming efficient mathematicians who are confident of their own thinking.

Learners need teachers who have the courage and wisdom to say:

> It's good that Theresa is drawing pictures to find the sum of those
> two numbers. Just think what she's learning and showing about her
> understanding. She's figured out that the problem requires joining
> quantities. She's getting a visual model of those quantities by drawing
> them out. She's getting practice with counting accurately. Now, what
> can I do, based on all that I've learned about Theresa, to help her
> become able to apply her knowledge of grouping by ten to this kind of
> problem? Does she just need more time solving similar problems?
> Would it help if she had more opportunities to see strategies that other,
> more advanced children are using? Is she ready for me to nudge her with
> a question about tens and ones? How can I make sure that I validate all
> that Theresa is doing right now so that she continues to maintain the
> positive and enthusiastic attitude that is so important in promoting
> learning while providing her with support that will help her advance?

It can be difficult to trust that students can and will find ways to make sense of mathematics. It's hard to forgo leading students through a step-by-step solution method and, instead, step back to see how they go about making sense of problems. But when children have the chance to come up with their own strategies, they cement what they already know and sometimes construct new understandings for themselves. One of the side benefits of this approach is that teachers often deepen their own mathematical understandings as they have the opportunity to see how their students go about solving problems!

Research that supports teaching for understanding

There is growing evidence to suggest that providing children with problem-solving and communication skills is the best way to prepare them to do well on standardized tests. Craig D. Jerald (2006) cites studies in Chicago and Worcester, Massachusetts, that point in this direction. He concludes:

> It is time to overturn the common assumption that teaching to the
> test is the only option schools have when faced with high-stakes
> testing. Overreliance on "drill and kill" and test-preparation
> materials is not only unethical in the long term, but ineffective in the
> short-term. Because there really is no trade-off between good
> instruction and good test scores, this is that rare case when educators
> can have their cake and eat it, too. (5)

David Foster and Pedred Noyce (2004) have tied improved test scores, and more importantly, improved learning, to the work they have been doing through the Silicon Valley Mathematics Initiative (SVMI), a program that makes extensive use of formative assessments devised by the Mathematics Assessment Research Source (MARS). The assessments are based on problem-solving exercises that teachers use to deepen their own mathematical understanding and their awareness of their students' strengths and needs.

> The SVMI has been able to demonstrate to the satisfaction of superintendents and school local committees that high-quality professional development significantly enhances student achievement. District case studies show that students whose teachers participate in intensive SVMI professional development, including coaching and work with formative assessment, achieve higher averages on both the state math test and the MARS exam than students whose teachers who [sic] are less involved. As a result, districts have continued to invest in math professional development, coaching, and formative assessment. . . .
>   The performance of MAC [*Mathematics Assessment Collaborative*] district students on the STAR [*Standardized Test and Reporting*] exam has continued to rise. For example, while 53 percent of third-graders performed above the 50th percentile on the state test in 1998, 72 percent did so in 2002. There is similar growth in the other grades, with a minimum of 11 percent more students above the 50th percentile at each grade level. (11)

And finally, Wendy B. Sanchez and Nicole F. Ice (2004) list Alan H. Schoenfeld's (2002) conclusions about mathematics curricula and standardized testing:

1. On tests of basic skills, there are no significant performance differences between students who learn from traditional or reform curricula.

2. On tests of conceptual understanding and problem solving, students who learn from reform curricula consistently outperform students who learn from traditional curricula by a wide margin.

3. There is some encouraging evidence that reform curricula can narrow the performance gap between whites and underrepresented minorities.

Save the Bubbles for Later

We've decided that it's important to say no to the notion of asking students, beginning early in the year, to complete multiple-choice worksheets that are filled with the least comprehensible test items likely to appear on the test. This stance is based partly on our belief that a steady diet of narrowly geared test practice has the potential to backfire because of both boredom and missed opportunities for real learning to occur. We take the position that if the standardized test is a special and somewhat isolated event, students are more likely to take it seriously and put effort into it. Presenting the standardized test as a unique opportunity to show how much they've learned during the year can motivate students to do their best on the test.

We steadfastly believe teaching that is directed primarily toward having students fill in the right bubble on a test shortchanges children. Today's technology makes it simple to get the correct answer to a computational problem by pressing a few buttons. A well-rounded mathematics education requires opportunities for children to develop mathematical-logical knowledge so they are able to use terminology appropriately and understand why (and if!) an answer is correct. In addition, today's standardized tests are likely to be based on a broad range of state standards for mathematics, so a narrowly focused curriculum and/or test-preparation program is unlikely to achieve test results that hold steady as students grow older or are required to take different tests.

In our own teaching we've decide to save the practice sheets until later in the year and do just enough of them to make sure that our students have a chance to become familiar with the format of the standardized test. By then they have engaged in thinking about most of the concepts that they will encounter on the test. With just a little time dedicated to fitting their learning into the specialized structure of the test, they're ready to show their best thinking.

We encourage you to be positive, focus on what you are already doing for your students, and look for ways that you can improve instruction in the future. Instead of getting overly concerned about how your students will perform on the current year's test, consider trying something different. Tell yourself that testing will be an opportunity for your students to show how much they've learned during the course of the year. Rather than focus on the negative, keep your eye on the learning your students can achieve when they're given an opportunity to develop understanding over time. Taking this broad viewpoint is important because it's a reminder that the year is long and that you're likely to get further with your students if you begin the year getting to know their current level of understanding and planning instruction accordingly. It's more likely that your students will be ready for what's on the test if you help them build a foundation starting with where they currently are in their understanding and then continue to look for opportunities that will help them move on to more complex thinking.

It's our desire for our students to become problem solvers who understand and love mathematics for the fascinating subject that it is. Working toward that goal keeps our students engaged today and will open doors for them in the future. The rest of this book will help you strategize about how to prepare students for the rigors of testing without compromising the larger, more important goals of your mathematics program. Our goal is to help teachers learn to cope with the pressures that accompany high-stakes testing as they go about the business of providing a strong conceptual foundation in mathematics for their students.

Resources

Following are some additional resources that support teaching for understanding:

Foster, David, and Noyce, Pedred. 2004. *The Mathematics Assessment Collaborative: Performance Testing to Improve Instruction.* www.noycefdn.org/documents/MACPerformanceTesting.pdf.

Jerald, Craig D. 2006. *"Teach to the Test"? Just Say No.* Issue brief (July). Washington, DC: Center for Comprehensive School Reform and Improvement. www.centerforcsri.org/files/CenterIssueBriefJuly06.pdf.

Sanchez, Wendy B., and Ice, Nicole F. 2004, December. "Standards-Based Teaching and Test Preparation Are Not Mutually Exclusive." *News Bulletin of the National Council of Teachers of Mathematics.* www.nctm.org/news/content.aspx?id=632.

Schoenfeld, Alan H. 2002. "Making Mathematics Work for All Children: Issues of Standards, Testing, and Equity." *Educational Researcher* 3 (1), 13–25.

Schuster, Lainie. 2009. *A Month-to-Month Guide: Fourth-Grade Math.* Sausalito, CA: Math Solutions.

Chapter 2

Planning to Teach Well and Test Well

Having a yearlong plan for instruction that takes into account the need to be prepared for the year-end standardized test can create a much-needed sense of control. Getting this kind of planning accomplished early in the year leaves one free to focus on providing high-quality math instruction in the months ahead. It is useful to do three things as early as possible:

1. create a yearlong plan for teaching mathematics, based on best teaching practices and a deep understanding of state standards;

2. become familiar with the topics addressed on the standardized test that your students will be taking and find ways to incorporate those concepts into your teaching throughout the year; and

3. find or create materials for limited, but highly directed test preparation when it seems appropriate.

Outlining Your Yearlong Plan for Teaching Math

Before school begins, or very early in the year, sketch out a rough plan for teaching math throughout the school year. The initial purpose of this plan is to make sure that you've thought through what's important for your students to learn during the year and that you have allocated enough time to cover all the concepts in the strands of mathematics that are appropriate for your grade level. Later on, as you refine your plan, you may decide to include information you've gleaned from a careful examination of the standardized test your students will eventually take. For now the goal is to focus your thinking, in a broad outline, on what you hope your students will learn during the year and how you will schedule all the units of study.

Getting to know your state standards

One place to start is with the document that outlines the standards for your state. Your principal or curriculum director can help you find a copy if you don't already have one. Figure 2–1 outlines some things to consider as you study your grade-level standards closely.

* What major number concepts are covered during the year? How will you translate these concepts into units of study?

* In the number strand, how is computation handled? Is it "naked" computation (that is, devoid of context) or embedded in measurement problems, money problems, and/or story problems?

* What knowledge or application of terminology is included in geometry, statistics, and probability, and other nonnumber strands?

* Are there standards that require knowledge of multiple representations? For example, does a standard require a student to look at an expression and determine its matching graph or to match a T-chart to its corresponding graph?

* Are there standards that ask students to look for patterns or use their knowledge of inverse operations to check a given answer?

* Which standards are introduced at your grade level? Which should be mastered at your grade level?

* If there are standards that don't seem like a good match for the developmental level of your students, is there a way to teach them that will make them more accessible for your class?

FIGURE 2–1   Get to know your state's grade-level standards.

It's also useful to look at the standards for the grade levels below and above yours. Looking back will give you a sense of what your students have previously experienced. For example, if your students are to learn about multiplication, it might be helpful to know if they have had experience with skip-counting, repeated addition, or no related experience at all. Looking ahead a grade level can give you a sense of where your children are headed. With this information you can decide to provide reinforcement of skills and knowledge they will need in subsequent years.

Getting ideas from other sources

District guidelines, if they are based on state standards and are well written, can help you interpret the standards more clearly. Refer also to the website of the National Council of Teachers of Mathematics. Reviewing the *Curriculum Focal Points for Prekindergarten Through Grade 8 Mathematics* (2006) can be helpful when creating a broad outline for the year. For now, this outline should represent your dream curriculum—what you really think is important for your students to learn. So feel free to include all of the knowledge about teaching children that you have acquired through your own experiences as a teacher. It is important to have a clear vision of what you think is important and appropriate for your students, but you may need to modify your plan as you gain additional information and experience.

Choosing teaching resources and integrating your textbook

Once you know the concepts that need to be included in your teaching program, think through which math resources include activities that are most appropriate for your units of study. You'll find suggested resources in this book and may have favorites of you own.

If your district requires you to use a textbook that has a different emphasis than you would choose on your own, you may also need to do some creative planning. Ideally you'll find ways to teach the concepts covered by the textbook that will allow your children to construct understanding about those concepts. For example, your emphasis may shift from teaching students the standard algorithm for addition to developing place-value concepts that enable students to add double-digit numbers accurately and efficiently. To show that your children have learned the concept and to provide added practice, you could have students complete some pages of the text. Keep in mind that children do not need to do every item on every page of the textbook to show that they understand the underlying mathematics presented on the page.

One idea is to assign a textbook page with a rule that defines which problems students must work on: *Do only the problems with a sum of more than fifty* or *Do only the problems that have an answer that is an odd number.* These kinds of assignments encourage students to estimate and thus think about the reasonableness of an answer, skills that are useful in both real life and test taking.

Examples of yearlong plans

Here are some examples of what a month-by-month plan might look like at two different grade levels:

Second Grade

- *September:* Create a classroom environment that encourages respect, risk taking, discussion, and explanation of problem solutions. Give students time to become familiar with materials, including how they are used and cared for. Introduce daily number talks about the number of the day (*Today's Number*), and use this activity throughout the year to provide emphasis and practice on whatever concept is currently being studied. Start partner work with card games that provide practice with single-digit combinations.

- *October and November:* Do number work with an emphasis on combinations for ten, doubles, multiples of two, five, and ten, and finally building to number sense with larger numbers (including story problems). Focus on decomposing small and large numbers, relative magnitude of numbers, and number relationships. Make sure to include work with money, learning coin values and names.

- *December:* Focus on data analysis. Emphasize collecting, organizing, and interpreting data.

- *January:* Focus on geometry. Emphasize classifying shapes and spatial problem solving that involves composing and decomposing shapes and basic shape vocabulary.

- *February and March:* Return to number with an emphasis on solving double-digit addition and subtraction story problems.

- *April:* Focus on probability. Include concepts about the likelihood of events, fair games, and using data to predict outcomes. Also review all basic facts.

- *May:* Focus on linear measurement. Emphasize iteration, the importance of equal-length units, and the inverse relationship between the size of unit and the number of units needed to measure. If there's time, create sand timers and develop notions about duration.

Fifth Grade

- *September:* Create a classroom environment that encourages respect, risk taking, discussion, and explanation of problem solutions. Begin the month with activities that focus on multiplication, factors, multiples, and number theory (odd and even, prime and composite). Expand these ideas into a unit on algebraic reasoning with an emphasis on patterns and functions to set the stage for integrating algebra and searching for patterns throughout the year.

- *October and November:* Begin the concept development of fractions, decimals, and percents and their relationship.

- *November:* Explore geometry, including the relationship of two-dimensional shapes to three-dimensional shapes and the properties of polyhedral solids.

- *December:* Begin a division unit to develop understanding of models for division, place value, properties, and the relationship of division to multiplication.

- *January:* Continue the division unit with an emphasis on developing fluency with procedures and problem contexts.

- *February and March:* Concentrate on addition and subtraction of fractions with unlike denominators and working with decimal models, percents, place value, and properties to add and subtract decimals.

- *April:* Explore measurement with a focus on area, surface area, and volume. Return to algebra, focusing on writing and solving simple equations and inequalities, creating graphs of simple equations, and multiple representations.

- *May:* Focus on data analysis. Have students apply their understanding of whole numbers, fractions, and decimals as they construct and analyze double-bar and double-line graphs and use ordered pairs on coordinate grids.

- *June:* Revisit multiplication and division, emphasizing division proficiency and using multiplication and division to solve problems.

Familiarizing Yourself with the Test

Once you have a basic math plan for the year, you may find that it needs to be modified as you become more familiar with the standardized test your students will take later in the year. Becoming familiar with the test includes making sense of the test for yourself, focusing on the language of the test, and deciding how this knowledge might affect what you teach. Developing this knowledge early in the year allows you to be able to incorporate it into your yearlong curriculum. The goal is not to know the specific test items for the current test, but to have a sense of the concepts that the test is likely to cover and how those concepts will be interpreted in test form. You may also find mathematical areas included in the test that you didn't include in your original plan and will need to make decisions about how best to deal with those areas.

Researching your test
All the information you need to research your state test may be at your school site already. Your principal is likely to have copies of sample test items and test-preparation materials and may be eager to help you get started on becoming familiar with the test at your grade level. If not, there may be a curriculum director or colleague who has materials that will be helpful. One way to make sure that you're gathering information that will be accurate, and therefore useful to your students, is to look at what your state department of education has posted on its website. In many states you can go online to find released test items—items that were on the test in years past. The easiest way to access the items is to use a search engine such as Yahoo! or Google and type in the words "released test items [your state or the name of your standardized test]." Released test items will give you a good feel for what your students will be asked to know, which can help you refine your yearlong planning. It is helpful to see an example of what the standard, as conceived by the state, looks like when it becomes a test item. Some states, like California, provide side-by-side information about standards and test items. For each grade level, all state math standards are listed, followed by related former test items. (See Figure 2–2.) Following the released test items is a table that correlates each with the appropriate math standard.

This information clarifies the standard and provides a greater sense of what will be expected of your students. However, the website containing this item includes a disclaimer:

> This is a sample of California State Test questions. This is NOT an
> operational test form. Test scores cannot be projected based on
> performance on released test items.
> (www.cde.ca.gov/ta/tg/sr/css05rtq.asp)

This caveat is an important reminder that it doesn't work to teach only to the specific released items. But you can use this information to develop a

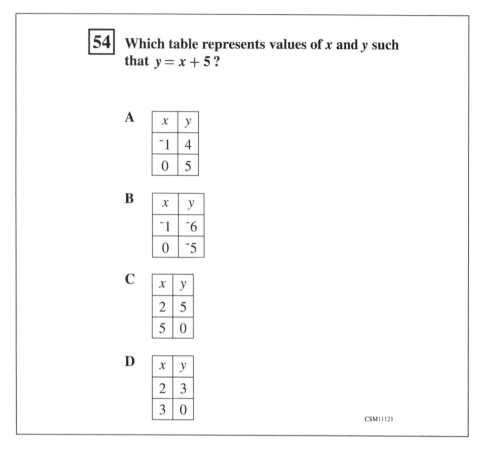

54 Which table represents values of x and y such that $y = x + 5$?

A

x	y
⁻1	4
0	5

B

x	y
⁻1	⁻6
0	⁻5

C

x	y
2	5
5	0

D

x	y
2	3
3	0

CSM11121

FIGURE 2–2   One of California's 2005 Grade 5 released test items for Standard 5AF1.5: "Solve problems involving linear functions with integer values; write the equation; and graph the resulting ordered pairs on integers grid."

broad understanding of your state standards and how those standards can appear in test format. Some states also post information about the percentage of students who answered each released test item correctly for a given testing year, indicating the kinds of questions that have been particularly difficult for your grade level.

Examining the practice test book critically

To further familiarize yourself with the test, you can peruse any practice test booklets that your school district has made available. Check to see if the test-prep materials are a close match in format and language to the test that your students will be taking by referring to the released test items you found on your state department's website. If the practice books are not a match for the test that you'll be administering, it's probably best to disregard them. And even if they are a close match, they should not become the basis of your math program. Later in this chapter and in Chapter 8 you'll find suggestions for creating and using practice test books wisely—and sparingly—so you can spend most of your teaching time helping your students develop conceptual understanding they can apply to real life *and* to testing situations.

Examining the test in order to make wise teaching decisions

As you begin to examine the released test items and get a feel for what the test will include, it is common to feel overwhelmed by the sheer volume of the material that a test covers. Take a big breath and, if possible, find a colleague to help examine the material. It's likely that you actually cover many of the concepts included in the test, but that you use different language. Students often make errors because the phrasing of a test item is unfamiliar. By noting unfamiliar language, you can help your students build bridges between their mathematical knowledge and the test items. Knowing the language of the test gives you many opportunities throughout the year to incorporate that language as you teach mathematical concepts so your students will be able to interpret test questions accurately.

Depending on the state test, you may see a few items that initially seem to require a solution method based on one particular algorithm. Remember that it's possible to solve many mathematical problems in ways that are unconventional but are accurate and efficient—even in a testing situation. If your students are given the opportunity to think about problems in ways that make sense to them throughout the year, they can use their own methods for solving problems on the test. Because so many of us were taught mathematics in a rigid way, we tend to look at the problems on the test and revert back to our own experience as test takers. In those days we may have had only memorized algorithms to draw on. A program based on teaching for understanding gives students many opportunities to create a variety of methods to use when solving problems. Later in the book, you'll find alternative algorithms that your students can use to solve test items. You'll also find suggestions for how to provide opportunities for your students to examine the types of problems that they'll be encountering on the test and to think through ways they might apply their understandings to solve those problems.

Incorporating Your Test Findings into Your Yearlong Plan

Once you know what's on the test, look for ways to incorporate this information into your daily teaching. Here's an example of an item that initially seemed more difficult than it actually is. A second-grade teacher found that her students were going to come across this type of problem on the test:

$$54 + 68 = 68 + \underline{\quad}$$

She knew that this format might perplex her children. To help them get beyond feeling confused by this presentation, she provided them with some focused experiences working with the ideas inherent in this type of problem. In this particular instance, the teacher already did a daily routine during which her students wrote equations for the number of the day, an exercise that gave students many opportunities to work on ideas of equality, including the commutative property. On most days the daily number routine was based on examining equations that students created, providing time for them to share their equations and justify their thinking, and checking whether they agreed or disagreed with each other's ideas. But on Day 126, after the class had found ways to prove that $59 + 67 = 126$ (an equation offered by a student), the teacher introduced this question:

$59 + 67 = 67 + \underline{\quad}$ *What number should go in the blank to make a true equation?*

A discussion about this question helped students become aware that even though there was an addition sign in the mathematical expression, the answer could be determined with logic rather than computation. Guided discussion helped students see that although they knew that $59 + 67 = 126$, they could use their knowledge of the commutative property of addition to come up with the answer to the question without doing the computation. If the teacher had been unaware that this type of problem could be on the test, she may have passed up an opportunity to have a rich mathematical discussion and also would have lost an opportunity to better prepare her students for the test.

Introducing relevant vocabulary

Your research will inform you about the specific mathematical vocabulary your students will be encountering on the test. When you know the terminology used on the test, you can look for ways to use that vocabulary throughout the year as you go about the business of teaching for understanding. For instance, if your children are going to encounter questions about *equilateral triangles,* you can make sure to use this term in context, for example when you do geometry lessons using the green triangular pattern blocks.

If the test you'll be administering has particular language associated with concepts, it helps to make the language accessible to your students by using it frequently. It's preferable to start with a lesson designed to deepen mathematical understanding, making sure to use relevant vocabulary when appropriate, rather than design a lesson focused primarily on the acquisition of the language.

Working on difficult concepts

There may be a few areas on the test that are a poor match for your students in terms of understanding, but that you can't ignore. Consider, for example, how one second-grade teacher in California dealt with such a situation. Many second-grade teachers have a gut feeling that fractions are not a great cognitive match for their students. And yet, the standardized test had several questions that the test makers assumed would offer clues about how knowledgeable students were about fractions. (See Figure 2–3.) There were several variations on this item, including some with $\frac{6}{6}$ as the correct answer. Because there were so many items dealing with fractions, they couldn't simply be overlooked.

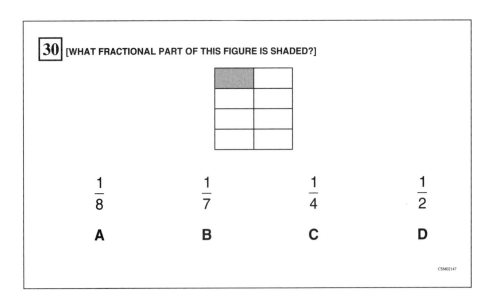

FIGURE 2–3   One of California's 2003 Grade 2 released test items.

The teacher decided she needed to design a series of lessons that would help students feel capable and confident when faced with these problems. She explained:

> I designed a lesson with red and yellow Unifix cubes that exposed my students to the notion that if there are two cubes, one being yellow and one red, we say that one out of two is yellow, and that relationship can be written as $\frac{1}{2}$. I went on to have everyone create a set of six cubes that had two yellow cubes and four reds and said, "In this group, two out of six are yellow. That's written as $\frac{2}{6}$." Eventually volunteers were asked to write the correct fraction on the board as we looked at other similar situations using cubes. At another time, I talked about how my family had eaten six out of six pieces of pizza and wrote on the board $\frac{6}{6} = 1$ *whole pizza*.
>
> As I taught the lessons I labeled them. *What You Need to Know About Second-Grade Fractions* and spent a minimal amount of time on them. I felt justified in doing these lessons because they helped my students feel confident and capable when approaching these items on the test. If I hadn't prepared my students in this somewhat superficial way, my whole math program could have come under fire.

It's important to note that, although the students may have come out of these lessons with a somewhat superficial understanding of fractions, the activities were designed so that they would not confuse the students. The children had a chance to use manipulative materials and to draw on their knowledge of pattern as they learned a little about fraction notation. The teacher avoided teaching by telling as much as possible, and she made sure not to veer into teaching an incomprehensible algorithm that might confuse students and undermine their confidence in their own thinking. Instead she kept the work narrowly focused on what her students needed to know to be successful on the test and wasted as little teaching time as possible.

You may find that a few items on the test appear to be conceptually too difficult for many or even most of your children. Often the difficulty comes from the magnitude of numbers involved in the problems, such as asking second graders to solve problems with three-digit numbers. Don't plan to gear your teaching to this most difficult level of achievement. Instead, focus on double-digit numbers throughout the year, saving problems with larger numbers until shortly before the testing period. By then, the solid foundation your students have achieved may allow them to tackle these larger numbers with a better chance of success. Remind yourself, too, that makers of standardized tests may purposefully include very difficult items in order to achieve a spread of scores among test takers, and that not all students are expected to mark every test item correctly.

Organizing and refining your plan

As you become familiar with the test, it may help to make a list of how this familiarity might affect your teaching, possibly dividing the material as follows:

- *Unfamiliar formats and linguistic constructions* that might trip up your students, even though they actually know the underlying mathematical concepts. You will need to decide when to introduce this material, incorporating it whenever possible into lessons you already have planned for your students and having the goal of using the ideas to deepen your students' understanding of important concepts.

- *Vocabulary words* you can introduce in your day-to-day teaching. It helps to think through lessons that give your children a chance to learn the vocabulary within the context of meaningful mathematics learning.

- *Concepts that you feel uncomfortable overlooking because there are so many test questions related to them.* You may want to think through how you will teach these concepts in a narrowly focused way without confusing your students or spending too much valuable teaching time on them. It's best to save this teaching until later in the year since it's likely to be short-lived in your students' minds.

- *Concepts that you plan to focus* most of your attention on throughout the year.

You might want to create a set of index cards, one for each of the test concepts that you plan to introduce to your students during the year. Use these cards to get started on planning how you'll fit the teaching of these concepts into your yearlong math program. Refer to the list occasionally so that you'll be attuned to appropriate opportunities for including them in your daily teaching.

You may also want to take a look at last year's test results. Noting areas of weakness in previous years' test scores may help you pinpoint areas of the curriculum that need special attention. Unfortunately it isn't always easy to look at test result reports and know with any precision what they refer to. You may need to do some detective work, perusing past tests, to get a feel for what each category in the report actually refers to. Any cross-references between standards and released test items that you found on your state's website can help with this endeavor.

You may now want to refine your yearlong plan for mathematics, taking into account what you have learned about the standardized test. This is a good time to expand old units of study to include new ways of looking at a particular concept, including specific mathematical vocabulary that your students will encounter on the test, and to pencil in new units of study if necessary.

A Revised Second-Grade Plan

Additions to the previous plan are in italics. This plan assumes that testing takes place in mid-May.

- *September:* Create a classroom environment that encourages respect, risk taking, discussion, and explanation of problem solutions. Give students time to become familiar with materials, including how they are used and cared for. Introduce daily number talks about the number of the day (*Today's Number*), and use this activity throughout the year to provide emphasis and practice on whatever concept is currently being studied. *Make sure to use this activity to discuss some of the many algebraic concepts about equality that students will be expected to understand for the test. Include class discussions around true-or-false statements for this same purpose.* Start partner work with card games that provide practice with single-digit combinations. *Try to include some games that involve probability since there will be little or no time for the unit originally planned for the spring.*

- *October and November:* Do some number work with an emphasis on combinations for ten, doubles, multiples of two, five, and ten, and finally building to number sense with larger numbers (including story problems). Focus on decomposing small and large numbers, relative magnitude of numbers, and number relationships. Make sure to include work with money, learning coin values and names. *Teach the appropriate way to write money values with mathematical symbols. Don't forget to have the children look at smaller-than-real-life diagrams of coins they will have to recognize on the test.*

- *December:* Focus on data analysis. Emphasize collecting, organizing, and interpreting data. *Include some opportunities to read the kinds of graphs that will be on the test. Make sure to create some bar graphs with only even numbers on the scale. Talk about why a graph maker might choose to have each item on the graph stand for two or five items.*

- *January:* Focus on geometry. Emphasize classifying shapes and spatial problem solving that involves composing and decomposing shapes. *Make sure to include test vocabulary such as* vertices, edges, *and* angles. *Include work with diagrams of three-dimensional shapes so students are prepared to decipher them on the test. Look at how geometry might lead to some rudimentary understanding about fractions.*

- *February and March:* Return to number with an emphasis on solving double-digit addition and subtraction story problems. *Continue to use* Today's Number *activities to discuss many of the test-item formats that relate to commutativity and other algebraic concepts covered on the test.*

- *April: Forego the probability unit. Instead focus on multiplication, fractions, and measurement. Introduce multiplication as repeated addition, do the second-grade fractions unit, and also take a brief look at the measurement ideas that are on the test. Use the last week of the month to introduce bubbling in and other oddities of the test using the test-prep books* [more on this in Chapter 8]. *Start using multiple-choice formats for the* Today's Number *activities.*

- *May: Continue using my teacher-made test-prep books. Administer the standardized test.* After the testing period, begin focusing on linear measurement in depth. Complete the unit in June, emphasizing iteration, the importance of equal-length units, and the inverse relationship between the size of unit and the number of units needed to measure.

The multiplication unit noted in April is a unit that needed to be added specifically because of the particular standardized test this teacher's students were required to take. When she had taught second grade in years past, she'd assumed that third grade was the appropriate year to introduce multiplication. When she realized that many items on the new test would require some knowledge of multiplication, she knew she needed to make some time for her students to explore this operation in a meaningful way. Although multiplication notation hadn't been part of her curriculum in the past, she felt that exploring basic concepts about multiplication could be a good cognitive match for her second graders and could be based on the work they would do in the fall with looking at multiples of numbers. She decided to place the multiplication unit later in the year so that her students could draw on all the work they would have done with number in both the fall and the early spring. It was important to know early in the year that she needed to work this unit into her math program so that she could set aside adequate time for it. She also needed to give herself time to search out multiplication activities that would be age appropriate for second graders. She developed the unit by modifying the first of several activities in an excellent third-grade unit of study. The long-term planning that she did left her feeling that she was providing meaningful, age-appropriate mathematics that added to her students' general knowledge about number, as well as experiences that would be helpful to them as test takers.

Your review of released test items may give you a sense of similar units of study that you will need to plan for your students. If there are units of study that you haven't taught in the past, but will need to introduce to your students, you will probably want to begin planning for them early. Joining forces with a colleague who can help you plan your course of study can be very useful.

Now, take another deep breath and remind yourself of two things:

- The good mathematics instruction that you provide throughout the year is going to enable your students to think through many of the test items.

- As the testing period approaches, you can choose to do more focused instruction designed to help your students apply their mathematical knowledge to the testing situation and also know when it's appropriate to a make a best guess if they encounter a problem that is truly incomprehensible.

Putting your plan into action

With your plan for teaching math in hand, you'll be able to spend the bulk of the year focusing on the mathematics you've outlined. Now that you're prepared to weave concepts and vocabulary that will eventually appear on the test into your mathematics program, you can devote your time to providing an excellent problem-solving math curriculum to your students, knowing that you are also doing important test preparation throughout the year.

Preparing for Focused Test Preparation

You may feel comfortable with the idea of doing all your test preparation within the context of your regular teaching. On the other hand, especially if your students will be taking a standardized test for the first time, you may want to set aside a block of time in the period shortly before the test to give your students a chance to learn how to take a multiple-choice test. In either case you may also want to start thinking about the materials that you'll use when you introduce the test-formatted problems to your students. Gather these materials whenever you can find the time so they'll be ready to use when you need them.

Reworking test-preparation materials

You can begin by taking a careful look at any test-prep materials that your district provides. Make sure that these materials mirror the actual test your students will eventually take. If they're not a match, they will not be worth your students' time. You may then want to think about creating your own test-preparation booklets based on released items from previous tests, using some of the organizing principles suggested below. Even if you find ready-made materials that are a good match for the specific language and format of your test, you may want to modify them to suit your teaching needs.

Some districts provide test-prep materials that mirror the state test very closely. However, the concepts may appear in random order in these practice booklets. For instance, the first item in the booklet might be related to fractions, the second to multiplication, the third to addition, and the fourth could be another fraction item that is easier than the first item. This haphazard arrangement of items can befuddle students rather than help them prepare. Going through these booklets runs the risk of wearing students down by making them take the test twice rather than providing them with an opportunity to consolidate and refine learning.

But it's easy to cut the test booklets apart and sort the test items by mathematical strand or concept. You can then rearrange them by order of difficulty within each strand, and may choose to add additional items to smooth the transition from easier to harder concepts. The result might be one minitest booklet on whole numbers, another on fractions, another on geometry, and so on. Arranged in this more sensible manner, the materials become a set of useful teaching tools that can give students an opportunity to review important concepts, learn how to deal with the bubbling-in format of the test, and encounter the language that will be used in the actual test.

Because of copyright issues, you should avoid photocopying the test-prep items from any materials that state that you cannot copy them. Instead, use different numbers and/or graphics, but include the language and formats your students will encounter on the test. A less labor-consuming route is to simply print the released test items for your grade level. They are likely to be grouped by concept; if they aren't, get out your scissors! Try to find a colleague who will share this task with you and remind yourself that once you produce truly useful test-prep materials, you'll be able to use them year after year.

Empowering students

Knowing that you have prepared practice materials that are ready to be introduced when it seems most appropriate can allow you to relax and go about the more important job of providing students with a good mathematics program throughout the year. When the time comes, you can present these materials to your students so that they have the opportunity to learn the format and language of multiple-choice testing and also review many of the concepts covered during the year. Using these materials effectively can have the important added benefit of empowering students, reassuring them that they can be successful on the test. This is an invaluable side effect, since feeling confident going into a test is half the battle. See Chapter 8 for thoughts on using test-preparation materials effectively with your students if you chose to review math concepts in test format prior to the test.

Resources

Following are some additional resources that support teaching for understanding:

Bachman, Vicki. 2003. *A Month-to-Month Guide: First-Grade Math.* Sausalito, CA: Math Solutions.

Do the Math program. 2007. New York: Scholastic.

Litton, Nancy. 2003. *A Month-to-Month Guide: Second-Grade Math.* Sausalito, CA: Math Solutions.

National Council of Teachers of Mathematics (NCTM). 2006. *Curriculum Focal Points for Prekindergarten Through Grade 8 Mathematics: A Quest for Coherence.* Reston, VA: NCTM.

Parker, Ruth E. 1993. *Mathematical Power: Lessons from a Classroom.* Portsmouth, NH: Heinemann.

Ronfeldt, Suzy. 2003. *A Month-to-Month Guide: Third-Grade Math.* Sausalito, CA: Math Solutions.

Schuster, Lainie. 2009. *A Month-to-Month Guide: Fourth-Grade Math.* Sausalito, CA: Math Solutions.

II

Teaching Computation with Alternative Algorithms

Computation is a significant part of the state tests that our students take each year. To do well on these tests, students must know much more than computational procedures and memorized basic facts. Our purpose in the following computation chapters is to look at developing students' understanding of the four whole-number operations and how these understandings lead children to be prepared for and confident about taking state math tests. We do not explore fractions, decimals, percents, estimation, or the other strands. Our point is that using algorithms that are understood by students supports their mathematical growth in general and also leads to success on the standardized tests.

The test items and standards included in the following computation chapters come from test questions released by various states that are available on the Internet. Although we were unable to secure examples from all fifty states, the available tests and standards included have many commonalities that are likely to apply to all state tests. For example, most states that we researched have standards that address comparing and ordering numbers; applying basic facts; understanding place value; understanding addition and subtraction as inverse operations; understanding multiplication and division as inverse operations; seeing multiplication as repeated addition, arrays, and equal groups; and representing problem-solving situations in ways that indicate understanding of the mathematics inherent in a variety of story problems. How and in what grade level these understandings are tested vary, but many test questions are about understanding and relatively few are purely computational in nature.

The alternative algorithms we discuss help students build strong understanding of place value, the base ten number system, and relationships among the operations. They help students understand why the mathematics works and judge the reasonableness of solutions. Additionally, we have found that teaching for understanding using alternative algorithms often reduces the need for reteaching due to poorly understood or forgotten standard algorithms, thus allowing us to spend more time on other areas of math. Having the time to focus on the other strands of mathematics is important relative to test taking since number and operations questions including computation typically account for only approximately half the test. The other half of the questions involve algebra, functions, patterns, geometry, measurement, data analysis, and probability. Many of the questions about these ideas require understanding of the concepts as well as the vocabulary. In some cases, simple computation also may be involved.

The examples of alternative algorithms we offer here are intended to stimulate your thinking about how these ideas can support and enhance your students' mathematical understanding, their success on state tests, and their ongoing mathematics learning. To better understand where your students have been and to help support them in where they will be going, we suggest you read all of the chapters on computation. Keep in mind that although we examine some of the conceptual underpinnings of the algorithms and even list some of the ways that students go about making sense of these concepts, the chapters in this section do not provide a curriculum to be used in the classroom. For that purpose, at the end of each chapter, we offer a list of teaching resources that you might turn to for further support.

Chapter 3

Teaching and Testing Addition

Becoming competent with addition involves more than being able to follow a sequence of memorized steps to find a correct answer. It includes having a good understanding of our place-value system and being able to apply that understanding to complex situations. The basis for understanding our place-value system is the ability to unitize, to understand that ten ones is the same quantity as one ten. This concept is foundational to the understanding of all whole number operations.

To develop a better understanding of place value, children need many opportunities to count groups of objects by ones, twos, fives, and tens and to write the numeric symbols that match those quantities. Playing games that involve trading a group of ten individual units for a single object that has a value of ten units (unit cubes for longs, pennies for dimes, etc.) can also be helpful.

Activities that allow children to become familiar with the patterns on a 1–100 chart arranged in rows of ten can also develop awareness of the organization of our number system. Understanding what happens to any number when you add ten to it is vital to being able to eventually add and subtract quantities. The 1–100 chart can also help with this understanding because it shows the effect of adding ten visually as you move down each column.

Young mathematicians should have opportunities to decompose all the single-digit numbers and they should become very familiar with the combinations for ten. Knowing combinations for ten enables a child to come to understand that $18 + 2 = 20$ (since $8 + 2 = 10$), and eventually that $40 - 7 = 33$ (since $10 - 7 = 3$). Either a number line or a 1–100 chart can be useful in illustrating these relationships.

Giving children the time to develop place-value understandings is both vital and challenging in the current test-preparation environment prevalent in so many districts. Textbooks often give us the sense that if we don't push children into learning the standard algorithm, they are going to fall behind. In fact, just the opposite is true. When children are given the time to develop place-value understandings, a process that takes many years starting in the early grades and continuing through middle school, they develop the tools and understandings that will enable them to add and subtract increasingly larger numbers, using methods that work as well or better than the standard U.S. algorithm.

Developing an algorithm to quickly and efficiently add quantities together is important, but it's only part of what children need in order to be adept at dealing with real-life situations and test problems that involve joining sets and understanding of the relationships between sets. When students are given time and appropriate experiences, they develop not only the computational skills needed to be successful but also more complex conceptual understandings about the operation of addition. Deep understanding of addition supports students' future understanding of subtraction and other whole number operations, helping them become successful mathematicians.

The standard algorithm that students are generally taught first in the United States is the one for adding two double-digit numbers. It involves arranging the addends vertically, adding the ones, putting the ones down and carrying the tens, and then adding the tens. It's efficient and supplies the correct answer every time—if you remember to do the steps correctly:

$$\begin{array}{r} {\scriptstyle 1} \\ 65 \\ + \ 28 \\ \hline 93 \end{array}$$

Unfortunately, too many children are taught this algorithm before they truly understand place value, and they often get the wrong answer because they perform the algorithm incorrectly. The most common mistake involves adding the ones in the right-hand column, but then recording both the tens and the ones in the answer section, rather than carrying. When the tens are added their total is placed in the answer section as though they were hundreds instead of tens:

$$\begin{array}{r} 65 \\ + \ 28 \\ \hline 813 \end{array}$$

The high incidence of this mistake is a strong indicator that this procedure encourages students to focus on manipulating individual digits with little regard to the reasonableness of the resulting answer.

Teaching this algorithm too soon discourages the use of the place-value understandings that enable children to perform calculations with large numbers with accuracy and authority. It places a premium on memorizing the steps to the algorithm rather than focusing on the quantities involved. It's interesting to note that state standards and standardized tests provide us with reminders that place-value understandings are indeed important. Here's an example from the California third-grade curriculum; the standard 3NS1.5 reads: *Use expanded notation to represent numbers (e.g. 3,206 = 3,000 + 200 + 6).* (See Figure 3–1.)

To answer the question correctly, the test taker must be able to split numbers—take them apart and put them back together again in ways that show place-value understandings. It requires a multiplicity of understandings about our base ten number system, including the following:

- Knowing that the position of each digit is significant: 4,085 is a different quantity than 4,805 even though the two numbers have all the same digits.

- Recognizing the base ten nature of our number system. In this case, the 4 is in the thousands place, the 0 is in the hundreds place, the 8 is in the tens place, and the 5 is in the ones place. Moving from right to left, the value of each digit is ten times greater than the digit to the right.

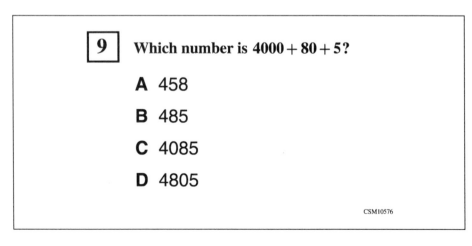

| **9** | **Which number is $4000 + 80 + 5$?** |

A 458

B 485

C 4085

D 4805

CSM10576

FIGURE 3–1   One of California's 2006 Grade 3 released test items.

- Understanding that the base ten structure of our number system requires us to be able to deal with the multiplicative nature of the number system. The correct answer in this case is based on knowing that 80 is 8×10, not 8×100.

- And finally, being aware of the additive nature of our system, which requires that you add $4,000 + 80 + 5$ to arrive at the correct total of $4,085$.

When they are able to understand these ideas, starting with two-digit numbers, children are able to draw on a natural, intuitive way of thinking about combining numbers and develop methods that accommodate their natural inclination to work from left to right when tackling a problem. Given the need to add two-digit numbers using methods that make sense to them based on a growing knowledge of place value, students often come up with some of the following algorithms:

$25 + 69 = \underline{\quad\quad}$

$20 + 60 = 80$

$5 + 9 = 14$

$80 + 14 = 94$

$$25 + 69 = \underline{\quad\quad}$$
$$20\quad 5\quad 60\quad 9$$
$$80\quad\quad 14$$
$$94$$

$25 + 69 = \underline{\quad\quad}$
$60\quad 9$
$5\quad 4$

$25 + 60 = 85$

$85 + 5 = 90$

$90 + 4 = 94$ $\quad$ or $85 + 9 = 94$

When discussing double-digit addition problems, you can help children invent these algorithms by modeling the expressions related to the problems in a horizontal fashion. For instance, consider this problem:

> *The room 5 second grade has collected $25 for the school project. The other second-grade class has collected $69. How much money have the second grades collected altogether?*

You could write $25 + 69 = $ ____ on the board to show students one way to conceptualize this problem. This orientation seems to help students see each quantity more readily and be able to focus on decomposing the numbers in the useful ways shown earlier.

When preparing for the test later in the year, you may need to discuss the vertical format for addition problems so your students understand what this arrangement represents. Then they can handily use their own algorithms to solve test problems efficiently and accurately, eventually being able to work with larger and larger quantities as they develop maturity and have more experiences. You may discover, in fact, that you never need to teach the standard algorithm in order for your students to do well on the standardized test. They will have their own solution methods and may even be able to do many of these calculations mentally. If you do decide to teach the standard method, we suggest that you hold off until your students can truly understand why it works. Better yet, when you feel the time is right, substitute the following vertical method:

$$
\begin{array}{r}
768 = 700 + 60 + 8 \\
+\,155 = 100 + 50 + 5 \\
\hline
800 \\
110 \\
\underline{13} \\
\hline
923
\end{array}
$$

This method will give your students practice aligning place-value columns as they continue to draw on place-value understandings. You'll find that, before long, students will not need to write out the expanded notation and will be able to compute quickly and accurately using this method.

A tool that you may want to introduce to your students when doing addition problems with large numbers is an open number line.

$$38 + 7 = \underline{\qquad}$$

$$167 + 128 = \underline{}$$

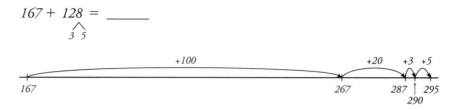

The strategy of using an open number line is not something that children usually invent on their own, but it does provide a linear representation that encourages students to use their growing sense of number. The number line is a visual model that helps them apply their ability to decompose numbers, use their knowledge about the relative magnitude of numbers, and apply place-value understandings to a variety of addition problems. Because it is graphic and linear, it allows children to reveal their thinking processes to themselves and others. Teachers can get a better picture of how students are thinking and help them move to increasingly efficient strategies. Other students can have access to the efficient strategies devised by classmates, becoming more efficient themselves. The open number line can be especially useful to students when working with subtraction, as you'll see when you read the next chapter.

Types of Addition Problems

In second and third grade, learners need experiences solving the following kinds of addition story problems

> **Join Problems (problems that involve *action verbs* that increase a quantity over time)**
>
> • Result unknown: *Mimi had 19 marbles. Her sister gave her 14 more. How many does she have now?* $19 + 14 = \underline{}$
>
> • Change unknown: *Mimi had 19 marbles. Her sister gave her some more. Now she has 33. How many marbles did her sister give her?* $19 + \underline{} = 33$
>
> • Initial quantity unknown: *Mimi had some marbles. Her sister gave her 14 more. Now she has 33. How many marbles did she have before her sister gave her the marbles?* $\underline{} + 19 = 33$
>
> **Part-Part-Whole Problems (problems that do not include action verbs and instead *establish a relationship* between a particular whole and its two parts)**
>
> • Whole unknown: *There were 19 red marbles and 14 yellow marbles in a jar. How many marbles were in the jar?* $19 + 14 = \underline{}$

- One part unknown: *There were 33 marbles in a jar. Nineteen of them were red. The others were yellow. How many yellow marbles were in the jar? 19 + ___ = 33*

Part-part-whole problems tend to be more difficult for young children because there is no implied action. It's important for students to solve this type of problem, initially using single-digit numbers and moving on to double- and triple-digit numbers as they become more sure of themselves. The value of solving part-part-whole problems is that students move beyond seeing addition only as action and start to develop a deeper understanding of the relationships between sets.

How Students Solve Addition Problems

In order to be able to invent and understand the methods shown earlier, students need the experiences and time to solve story problems that include first single digits, then double digits, and later larger numbers. In your classroom, young learners may progress through the following methods when solving addition problems with large numbers:

- modeling all
- counting on
- finding numeric solutions that make sense to them

Modeling all

Many second graders begin the year needing to model and count the entire quantity when solving a story problem such as this:

Mara had 15 stickers; Joan had 17. How many did they have altogether?

The modeling process might involve drawing all the stickers or using cubes to represent the set of fifteen and the set of seventeen. This method is obviously not efficient, but it serves the learner well. It offers an opportunity to develop a sense of the quantities and a clearer understanding of the relationship between the sets and the whole.

Counting on

Over time and with opportunities to participate in discussions with classmates who have already reached this stage, students move on to being able to hold the first quantity in their head, counting on from that number to determine the total. Students employing this method sometimes use fingers to keep track of the second quantity or record a double count:

1   2   3   4   5   6   7   8   9   10   11   12   13   14   15   16   17
(15) 16   17   18   19   20   21   22   23   24   25   26   27   28   29   30   31   32

Students who have reached this stage have come a little closer to being able to deal with quantities abstractly but are still building important understandings about quantities.

Finding numeric solutions

By the end of second grade or the beginning of third grade, children should have moved on to some of the algorithms shown on pages 34 and 35. If they haven't used the open number line method on their own, it may be a good time to teach it.

You can support your students in reaching the numeric stage by giving them opportunities to use a variety of manipulative materials such as cubes, tiles, and other counters, and tools such as ten frames, 1–100 charts, and number lines. You can scaffold their growth by providing experiences that promote understanding the following concepts and trying out the following strategies:

- understanding the meaning of addition

- decomposing one-digit and, later, larger numbers

- using the commutative property of addition

- learning and using combinations that add to ten

- using place-value exchanges in games: ten ones for one ten, ten tens for one hundred, and so on

- learning doubles and near-doubles relationships ($6 + 6 = 12$, so $6 + 7 = 13$)

- adding any one-digit number to 10

- combining two one-digit numbers by decomposing one of the numbers to make a 10 and seeing what spills over ($6 + 7 =$ ___ can be solved by decomposing the seven into a four and a three, and then recombining the numbers in this fashion: $6 + 4 = 10$ and $10 + 3 = 13$

- adding any one-digit number to any two-digit number by using a similar decomposing and recombining strategy to make the next 10 and see what spills over ($26 + 7 =$ ___ is thus thought of as $26 + 4 = 30$ and $30 + 3 = 33$)

- adding ten to any number

- adding multiples of ten to any number by counting ($24 + 40 =$ ___ is solved by thinking 34, 44, 54, 64)

- adding multiples of ten to any number using a known addition fact ($20 + 40 = 60$ because $2 + 4 = 6$)

- combining two-digit numbers by splitting each addend into its place-value parts and recombining the parts ($37 + 24 =$ ___ can be solved by adding $30 + 20 = 50$, $7 + 4 = 11$, and finally $50 + 11 = 61$—which requires mentally splitting eleven into ten and one more and thinking $50 + 10 + 1 = 61$ *or* by recombining $37 + 20 = 57$, $57 + 4 = 61$—which is accomplished by thinking $57 + 3 + 1 = 61$)

- using the above strategies to read, write, and add greater numbers

When looking at this list, it's important to remember that children do not have to be adept at all of these separate strategies or have a complete understanding of all the mathematical concepts before they are asked to solve addition problems. The act of solving problems in ways that make sense to the student, along with games, classroom discussions, and directed lessons, enables students to devise and understand increasingly efficient methods of solving addition problems. Chapin and Johnson write:

> In order to use addition and subtraction effectively, children must first attach meaning to these operations. One way for young children to do this is by manipulating concrete objects and connecting their actions to symbols. However, this is not the only way. They extend their understanding of situations involving addition and subtraction by solving word problems. (2006, 55)

Addition on Standardized Tests

When thinking about what students need to be successful as mathematicians and test takers, it can be instructive to look at the state standards. Doing so reminds us that students are expected to be competent not only at computation but also at problem solving. One of the third-grade Texas state standards reads:

> *3.15 C Select or develop an appropriate problem-solving strategy, including drawing a picture, looking for a pattern, systematic guessing and checking, acting it out, making a table, working a simpler problem, or working backwards to solve a problem.*

The following problem typifies how the state assesses this standard:

> *Anna, James, and Olivia are playing a number game. James has 16 points. Olivia has twice as many points as James. Anna has 5 fewer points*

than Olivia. Which shows the number of points that each person has?
Mark your answer.

A. Anna 13, James 16, Olivia 18

B. Anna 3, James 16, Olivia 8

C. Anna 27, James 16, Olivia 32

D. Anna 37, James 16, Olivia 32

Students who have had experience with a variety of story problems are more likely to be able to plan a strategy for solving a problem that requires careful reading and involves more than one step. To be successful with this problem, the student needs to double James's sixteen points to find out how many points Olivia has (thirty-two), and then subtract five from that total to arrive at Anna's number of points (twenty-seven). The computation should be easy for a third grader, but many students make incorrect choices because this type of problem requires students to untangle what the question is asking and to pursue an answer that isn't readily reached.

Even a bare-bones item will be more easily solved by a student who has been approaching mathematics through problem solving than by one who has memorized a standard algorithm and then spent most of her class time repeating the procedure over and over again. (See Figure 3–2.)

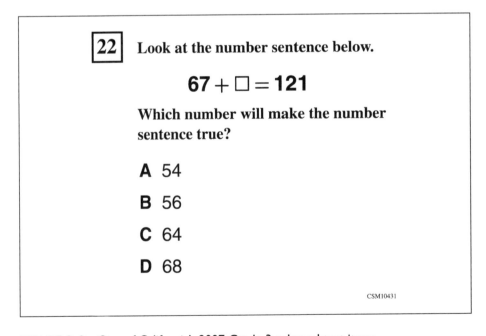

FIGURE 3–2   One of California's 2007 Grade 3 released test items.

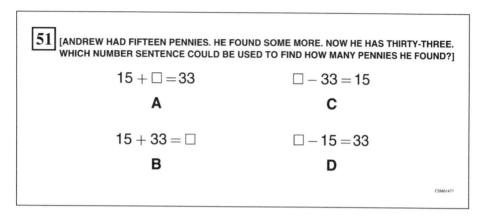

51 [ANDREW HAD FIFTEEN PENNIES. HE FOUND SOME MORE. NOW HE HAS THIRTY-THREE. WHICH NUMBER SENTENCE COULD BE USED TO FIND HOW MANY PENNIES HE FOUND?]

$$15 + \square = 33 \qquad\qquad \square - 33 = 15$$

A   C

$$15 + 33 = \square \qquad\qquad \square - 15 = 33$$

B   D

CSM01477

FIGURE 3–3 One of California's 2007 Grade 2 released test items.

A student who has been actively engaged in solving word problems with an unknown change should be able to solve this problem quickly and accurately. She will be familiar with situations that the number sentence represents and will not be thrown by finding a number missing in the middle of an equation. She'll be able to draw on past experience and solve the problem by counting up, possibly using an open number line, or by inserting some of the possible answers into the box to see which yields a total of 121, or by subtracting.

The same argument holds true for a released item from a 2007 second-grade test in California. (See Figure 3–3.)

This dizzying array of possible answers might at first stymie even a second grader with lots of problem-solving experience. But a child who has encountered many change-unknown problems will have had a chance to see equations similar to $15 + \square = 33$ used as models for representing this type of problem. He'll be much more likely to persevere in sorting out the incorrect answers and choosing the one that fits the story situation than students who aren't familiar with this representation.

Another payoff for developing deep understanding about addition is that students have both the conceptual underpinnings and the flexibility in their thinking to correctly answer the algebraic problems involving equality that are prevalent on many standardized tests. These include such formats as the following:

What number goes in the box to make this number sentence true?

$15 + 8 = \square + 15$

A. 7   C. 15

B. 8   D. 23

Which sign makes the number sentence true?

22 + 10 ___ 32

A. +   *C. >*

B. =   *D. <*

What other problem has the same answer as 4 + 2 + 6 = 12?

A. 6 + 4 + 3 = □

B. 12 + 6 + 2 = □

C. 4 + 12 + 6 = □

D. 2 + 4 + 6 = □

Without this kind of learning we end up with the following sad situation. On the 2003 National Assessment of Educational Progress (NAEP) test, only 34 percent of fourth graders got full credit for answering the next question correctly; another 23 percent received partial credit, leaving 43 percent of fourth graders nationwide missing the mark:

Jan entered four numbers less than 10 on his calculator. He forgot what his second and fourth numbers were. This is what he remembered doing.

8 + ___ − 7 + ___ = 10

List a pair of numbers that could have been the second and fourth numbers (partial credit).

List a different pair that could have been used for the second and fourth numbers (full credit).

There's more than one way to go about solving this problem. A student could reason that since $8 - 7 = 1$, the total of the missing two digits must be 9 in order to bring the total up to 10. The next step is to create a list of at least two pairs of single-digit numbers that add to 9:

9, 0   8, 1   7, 2   6, 3   5, 4

This method would result in getting full credit.

To get partial credit a student could use a guess-and-check method, plugging numbers into the blanks until a total of ten was achieved. A persistent problem solver might even use this method to come up with a second possible pair.

The poor results for this test item can't be traced back to poor computation skills because the problem is directed at fourth graders, who should be able to add and subtract single-digit number with ease. The culprit has to be a lack of problem-solving experiences that would have prepared more students to think through this problem.

And finally, here's another NAEP test item involving simple computation, which only 78 percent of the fourth graders taking the test in 2003 answered correctly:

On Thursday Becky made some popcorn balls.

On Friday she made 6 popcorn balls.

On Saturday she made 12 popcorn balls.

Becky took all 23 popcorn balls that she made to a party.

How many popcorn balls did she make on Thursday?

A. 5

B. 11

C. 17

D. 41

Spend a few moments thinking about the steps that could lead to the correct answer (five) and why so many fourth graders did not choose that answer. To be successful, a student could conceptualize this problem with the following number sentences:

6 + 12 + ___ = 23

or 23 − 6 − 12 = ___

or, after adding 6 + 12 to get 18, 23 − 18 = ___

What might prevent a fourth grader from using one of these solution strategies and then performing the correct computation to get the right answer?

A mathematics program that emphasizes memorizing algorithms seems much more likely to produce fourth graders who would be unsuccessful at solving this problem than does a mathematics program that encourages children to understand our number system and use those understandings to think about reasonable ways to solve multistep problems.

Advantages to a Problem-Solving Approach to Addition

Giving children the time and experiences they need to develop a deep understanding of addition has the following advantages:

- Students who understand what they're doing make fewer mistakes when solving problems in the classroom and on tests.

- Students who learn how to add using a problem-solving approach develop understandings about our place-value system that serve them well as they move on to other operations and to more complex mathematics in years to come.

- Students who solve problems in ways that make sense to them develop perseverance when problem solving and do not give up when they are presented with problems they have never before encountered.

- Students who understand addition in all its complexities can apply those understandings to many problems commonly found on standardized tests.

Resources: Place Value and Addition

Following are some additional resources that support teaching for understanding:

Carpenter, Thomas P., Megan Loef Franke, and Linda Levi. 2003. *Thinking Mathematically: Integrating Arithmetic and Algebra in Elementary School.* Portsmouth, NH: Heinemann.

Chapin, Suzanne, and Art Johnson. 2006. *Math Matters: Understanding the Math You Teach, Grades K–8.* 2d ed. Sausalito, CA: Math Solutions.

Economopoulous, Karen, and Susan Jo Russell. 1997. *Putting Together and Taking Apart.* Investigations in Number, Data, and Space series. Glenview, IL: Pearson.

Fosnot, Catherine Twomey, and Maarten Dolk. 2001. *Young Mathematicians at Work: Constructing Number Sense, Addition and Subtraction.* Portsmouth, NH: Heinemann.

Litton, Nancy. 2003. *A Month-to-Month Guide: Second-Grade Math.* Sausalito, CA: Math Solutions.

Ronfeldt, Suzy. 2003. *A Month-to-Month Guide: Third-Grade Math.* Sausalito, CA: Math Solutions.

Russell, Susan Jo, Karen Economopoulos, et al. 2008a. *Collections and Travel Stories: Addition, Subtraction, and The Number System, Grade 3.* Investigations in Number, Data, and Space series. Glenview, IL: Pearson.

———. 2008b. *Counting, Coins, and Combinations: Addition, Subtraction, and the Number System 1, Grade 2.* Investigations in Number, Data, and Space series. Glenview, IL: Pearson.

———. 2008c. *How Many Hundreds? How Many Miles? Addition, Subtraction, and The Number System, Grade 3.* Investigations in Number, Data, and Space series. Glenview, IL: Pearson.

———. 2008d. *How Many Tens? How Many Ones? Addition, Subtraction, and The Number System 3, Grade 2.* Investigations in Number, Data, and Space series. Glenview, IL: Pearson.

———. 2008e. *Partners, Teams, and Paper Clips: Addition, Subtraction, and The Number System 4, Grade 2.* Investigations in Number, Data, and Space series. Glenview, IL: Pearson.

———. 2008f. *Stickers, Number Strings, and Story Problems: Addition, Subtraction, and The Number System 2, Grade 2.* Investigations in Number, Data, and Space series. Glenview, IL: Pearson.

———. 2008g. *Trading Stickers, Combining Coins: Addition, Subtraction, and The Number System, Grade 3.* Investigations in Number, Data, and Space series. Glenview, IL: Pearson.

Scharton, Susan. 2005. *Teaching Number Sense, Grade 2.* Sausalito, CA: Math Solutions.

Tank, Bonnie, and Lynne Zolli. 2001. *Teaching Arithmetic: Lessons for Addition and Subtraction, Grades 2–3.* Sausalito, CA: Math Solutions.

Van de Walle, John. 2006. *Elementary and Middle School Mathematics: Teaching Developmentally.* 6th ed. Boston: Allyn and Bacon.

Wickett, Maryann, and Marilyn Burns. 2002. *Teaching Arithmetic: Lessons for Introducing Place Value, Grade 2.* Sausalito, CA: Math Solutions.

———. 2005. *Teaching Arithmetic: Lessons for Extending Place Value, Grade 3.* Sausalito, CA: Math Solutions.

Chapter 4

Teaching and Testing Subtraction

Subtraction presents new challenges to students. Although subtraction is the inverse of addition and can and should be taught concurrently with it, children often have a more advanced understanding of addition than of subtraction. Students need ample time to construct understandings about subtraction and the various types of problems that can be solved using it. Teaching subtraction concurrently with addition and building on and applying place-value knowledge to both operations will support students' understanding of the relationship between addition and subtraction and will increase their mathematical power.

The standard U.S. algorithm for subtraction is often confusing for children to follow. It involves arranging the numbers vertically, subtracting column by column starting with the ones on the right, and borrowing from the column to the immediate left if the digit in the subtrahend is larger than the digit in the minuend. This procedure results in the correct answer if you remember to do the steps correctly:

$$
\begin{array}{r}
{\scriptstyle 5\ 11\ 1} \\
6\,2\,6 \\
-\ 4\,3\,9 \\
\hline
1\,8\,7
\end{array}
$$

Students often have trouble remembering this complex procedure and, as with the standard U.S. algorithm for addition, they routinely make errors when trying to follow it. These errors suggest that students haven't used their number sense or understanding of place value. As soon as children lose sight of whether or not an answer makes sense, we lose them. It's critical that they have a way of determining whether their answers are reasonable or not. Students who do not understand the standard algorithm often end up just subtracting the smaller digit from the larger one in each column:

$$\begin{array}{r} 626 \\ -439 \\ \hline 213 \end{array}$$

Alternatively, if students are given both the time and the opportunity to apply their number sense to subtraction problems, eventually they will be able to solve subtraction problems using the following procedures:

$67 - 49 =$ _____
     ⋀
    40 9
      ⋀
     7 2

$67 - 40 = 27$

$27 - 7 = 20$

$20 - 2 = 18$

The open number line works equally well for larger quantities:

$478 - 269 =$ _____

Types of Subtraction Problems

For students to become truly proficient with subtraction, they need to construct understanding about the two major types of subtraction problems: *separate* and *compare* problems.

Separate problems involve actions that decrease a quantity:

- Result unknown: *Joe had 23 rocks. He lost 16 of them. How many does he have left?* $23 - 16 = $ ___

- Change unknown: *Joe had 23 rocks. He lost some of them. Now he has 7 rocks. How many did he lose?* $23 - $ ___ $= 7$

- Initial quantity unknown: *Joe had some rocks. He lost 16 of them. Now he has 7 rocks. How many did he start with?* ___ $- 16 = 7$

Compare problems, on the other hand, involve a comparison of two distinct quantities:

- Difference unknown: *Joe has 23 rocks. Luna has 7. How many more rocks does Joe have than Luna?* $23 - 7 = $ ___ *or* $7 + $ ___ $= 23$

- Smaller quantity unknown: *Joe has 23 rocks. He has 16 more rocks than Luna. How many rocks does Luna have?* $23 - 16 = $ ___ *or* $16 + $ ___ $= 23$

How Students Solve Subtraction Problems

As with addition, students need the opportunity to solve subtraction problems that include first single-digit numbers, followed by double-digit numbers, then larger numbers. Starting with smaller numbers allows the child to visualize familiar quantities in order to get a sense of how numbers relate to one another in various situations. This number sense can then be extended to increasingly larger numbers.

Students also need a chance to internalize the language of subtraction, such as what the word *difference* means. Working with story problems helps students understand this language and be able to apply their numeric understandings to a variety of problem situations. This kind of work prepares children for testing and for applying mathematics in real life.

Separate problems

When solving separate problems students might initially be most comfortable using any of the following strategies:

- modeling all
- counting backward
- finding numeric solutions like the ones shown on page 48.

Modeling all

Second and third graders might begin the year needing to use objects or pictures to represent the quantities in this type of problem:

> Joan had 25 beads. She gave 9 to her friend. How many beads does she
> have left?

A child using this strategy might count out twenty-five cubes, move nine of them away, and then count those that are left. Or she might draw twenty-five circles, cross off nine of them, and then count the ones that are left. This method helps the child get a clear picture of what it means to separate a part of the set from the whole.

Counting backward

To solve the beads problem, a student using this strategy would start with twenty-five and then count back nine:

$$1 \quad 2 \quad 3 \quad 4 \quad 5 \quad 6 \quad 7 \quad 8 \quad 9$$
$$\textcircled{25}\ 24\ 23\ 22\ 21\ 20\ 19\ 18\ 17\ 16$$

This method sometimes involves recording a double count, as shown above, or using fingers to keep track of counting back nine.

Finding numeric strategies

Numeric strategies are shown on page 48. It makes sense to help students learn to decompose numbers in ways that allow them to make use of equations or use a tool such as the open number line.

Compare problems

Compare problems present special challenges because they can be linguistically more diverse and, equally important, do not suggest any action. The language issue derives from the fact that there are many different things to compare: quantities (*more, less*), height (*taller than, shorter than*), temperature (*colder, warmer, hotter*), weight (*lighter, heavier*), and so on. Students need experience with the vocabulary that matches these different situations. They also need to work out in their own minds what it means to compare two sets.

Modeling

Students might need to use manipulatives to represent a compare problem such as this:

> Joan had 11 pennies; Albert had 9 pennies. How many more pennies did
> Joan have than Albert?

For example, a student could get out one set of eleven cubes and another set of nine. Then he could line the two sets up side by side to make it evident that there is a difference of two between the sets. Teachers can provide this kind of experience by creating class bar graphs and then asking questions about how the amount in one column on the graph *compares* with that in another column.

Alternatively, a student might count out nine cubes to represent Albert's pennies and then add two more cubes to make eleven, the amount that Joan had. Or the student might start with eleven cubes and note that by taking away two cubes, she is left with nine cubes, the number of pennies that Albert had.

Counting up or counting down

To solve the pennies problem, a student might reason: "I'll start at nine and then see how many more I need to get to eleven," or "I'll start at eleven and see how far away it is from nine by counting backward." Using fingers or some other way of keeping count, the student can arrive at the correct answer.

Finding numeric strategies

The various subtraction methods described above allow a child to construct his understanding about how two sets relate to one another. Then the child has the underpinnings needed to conceptualize problems and either decompose the original numbers into numbers that are easier to compute with or use an open number line to figure the answer.

It's important to note that not all children will need to work through all of these strategies with each of the two major types of subtraction problems. But all children do need to understand that subtraction is not always *take away*. For all children, working with compare problems has the advantage of helping students see the inverse relationship between addition and subtraction. This relationship is important for students to understand and is often tested on standardized tests.

Eventually we want students to be adept at solving a compare problem such as the following:

> *If the temperature is 72 degrees in Oakland and 89 degrees in Houston, what is the difference in temperature? Can you solve this problem by adding or subtracting?*

A complete answer would show that the student can solve the problem both ways, for example:

- Addition: $72 +$ ___ $= 89$

$8 + 9 = 17$

- Subtraction: $89 - 72 =$ ___

$10 + 7 = 17$

Students who have had these kinds of experiences in their mathematics program will understand the inverse relationship between addition and subtraction. They will know that they can confirm the answer to $253 - 108 = 145$ by adding ($145 + 108 = 253$), a situation that appears on standardized tests with some frequency.

Subtraction on Standardized Tests

Let's take a look at how subtraction plays out in standardized tests and how children fare when asked to solve problems that can be solved by subtracting.

The following item from the National Assessment of Educational Progress (NAEP) fourth-grade test has a Moderate Complexity rating, a category described as requiring:

A response that goes beyond the habitual, is not specified, and ordinarily has more than a single step. The student is expected to decide what to do, using informal methods of reasoning and problem-solving strategies, and to bring together skill and knowledge from various domains.

The item reads:

The Ben Franklin Bridge was 75 years old in 2001. In what year was the bridge 50 years old?

A. *1951*

B. *1976*

C. *1984*

D. *1986*

A fourth grader with good number sense, who understands the mathematical relationships implicit in this problem, could reason:

> The bridge was 75 years old in 2001 but I need to figure out when it was only 50 years old. Since $75 - 50 = 25$ I need to figure out what year it was 25 years before 2001. I could subtract 25 years from 2001. But I'll make the problem easier on myself by thinking about $2000 - 25$. That would be 1975—and then I have to add 1, since I actually needed to start with 2001. 1976 is the correct answer.

The computation involved in this problem should not be particularly difficult for fourth graders. But children who spend most of their mathematical studies learning algorithms might not be able to unpack what this question is asking. And if they can't understand the mathematical relationships involved in thinking about the problem, their computational ability alone is going to fail them.

Sadly, the 2007 National Performance Results for fourth graders indicates that 36 percent got the correct answer, a whopping 63 percent chose an incorrect answer, with the item omitted 1 percent of the time.

A lack of experience with comparison problems may explain why our research indicates that roughly 30 percent of students choose the incorrect response on problems, such as the following, that appear routinely on third-grade standardized tests throughout the country:

> *This year 345 students attend Melrose School. Last year there were 329 students enrolled. How many more students are there at Melrose this year than last year?*
>
> *A. 14*
>
> *B. 16*
>
> *C. 24*
>
> *D. 26*

> *On Monday 237 children bought lunch in the school cafeteria. On Tuesday only 186 students bought their lunches. How many more students bought lunch in the cafeteria on Monday than Tuesday?*
>
> *A. 131*   *C. 51*
>
> *B. 61*   *D. 151*

Here's another type of compare problem that appears on standardized tests:

> *Janelle is 48 inches tall. Her mother is 67 inches tall. What number sentence can be used to find out how much taller Janelle's mother is than Janelle?*
>
> A. $67 - 48 =$ _____
>
> B. $67 \div 48 =$ _____
>
> C. $67 \times 48 =$ _____
>
> D. $67 + 48 =$ _____

In this case, the student does not even need to perform the calculation to mark the correct answer. Instead, she needs to know that the problem can be solved by finding the difference between the two numbers and that the difference can be mathematically conceptualized by a subtraction sentence.

Some test items require that the student conceptualize the problem as a comparison between two amounts of money. (See Figure 4–1.) A student who is well versed in such problems could compare just the penny amounts, noting that the difference is twenty-four cents, leaving A as the only possible answer. An open number line would be an effective tool for solving this problem; students could use it to either count up from forty-seven to seventy-one or count down from seventy-one to forty-seven:

$20 + 3 + 1 = 24$

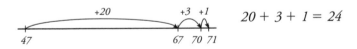

$20 + 3 + 1 = 24$

$20 + 4 = 24$

Many state tests have an occasional straight computation problem. (See Figure 4–2.)

15 **Reggie compared the prices of two radios. The table below shows the prices.**

Cost of Radios

Brand	Cost
A	$31.47
B	$34.71

How much more does Brand B cost than Brand A?

A $3.24

B $3.26

C $3.34

D $3.36

CSM02174

FIGURE 4–1   One of California's 2003 Grade 3 released test items.

22                    $5894 - 2608 =$

A   3276

B   3286

C   3294

D   3296

CSM01152

FIGURE 4–2   One of California's 2003 Grade 4 released test items.

An open number line also works well for this type of problem, allowing the students who have place-value understanding to create moves that eventually land at the correct answer:

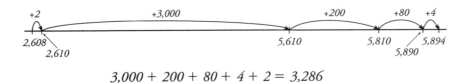

$$3,000 + 200 + 80 + 4 + 2 = 3,286$$

Fourth graders who have developed strong place-value understanding are unlikely to be among the 56 percent of students who failed to answer the following question correctly on the 2005 NAEP test:

A club needs to sell 625 tickets. If it has already sold 184 tickets to adults and 80 tickets to children, how many more does it need to sell?

Answer: _____

This multistep problem requires the test taker to conceptualize the situation as one involving comparison. First the student needs to add 184 and 80 tickets to find out the total tickets that have already been sold—264—a task that should be easy for a fourth grader. Then the student must determine the difference between 264 and 625. The standard algorithm could be used to determine the correct answer, but an open number line works equally well:

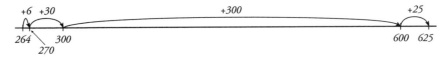

$$300 + 30 + 25 + 6 = 361$$

The open number line method also has the advantage of giving students confidence that their answer is correct, as they see how the answer is related to the other numbers in the problem. It's important that students routinely have an awareness that their answers can and do make sense so that they avoid the pitfall of accepting nonsense answers resulting from procedural mistakes.

By fourth grade it should be easy for students to see that $30 + 25 = 55$ and that $55 + 6 = 61$. Combine 61 with 300 and the answer is 361. When you see this process written out it seems long, but students who have had many experiences combining numbers in this way can do the math mentally, quickly and efficiently. In fact, fourth-grade students should be able to make even bigger jumps on the number line (jumping from 264 to 300 in one jump, for instance), making the process even more streamlined.

Advantages to a Problem-Solving Approach to Subtraction

Giving children the time and experiences needed to understand subtraction has the following advantages:

- It allows them to use what they know about addition to build understandings about subtraction.
- It helps them understand the relationship between addition and subtraction.
- It provides opportunities for students to continue building their knowledge of place value.
- It supports student's ability to solve multistep problems and develop the language of subtraction.
- It develops students' ability to use their sense-making skills at all times, including in testing situations.

Resources

Since addition and subtraction are inverse relationships, they are generally covered in the same resources. See the "Resources" section in Chapter 3 for suggestions.

Chapter 5

Teaching and Testing Multiplication

As students move from their study of addition and subtraction to multiplication and division, a major shift in thinking and understanding needs to occur. Up until now, students have been using additive reasoning, a natural, intuitive way of thinking about combining, taking away, and comparing numbers. When children reason additively, they consider each object individually—that is, they see the number three as three discrete, individual objects that can be operated on. When reasoning multiplicatively, three can be thought of as a unit of three rather than three discrete objects.

Consider the following two problems:

$4 + 3$

4×3

These two problems contain the same numbers, but the operation sign changes the meaning of the numbers. In the first problem, an example of additive reasoning, the addition sign indicates that four objects are to be combined with three other objects. In the second problem, an example of multiplicative reasoning, the multiplication sign indicates that there are four groups, or sets, of three objects. The outcomes of these two problems are of course very different.

While additive reasoning develops naturally for most children, multiplicative reasoning does not. Initially, many students use counting or addition to solve multiplication problems. For example, to solve 4×3, read as "four groups of three," a child might count by ones, using his fingers to help keep track by putting up three fingers four times, ending on twelve, or he might add 3 + 3 + 3 + 3. In both of these cases, the student is showing emerging understanding of multiplicative thinking because he recognizes that the 4 indicates a number of groups and the 3 is the number within the groups. This is a big shift from thinking of the 4 as four discrete objects to be combined with the other discrete objects. Teaching that links this early understanding to the language and notation of multiplication will help develop multiplicative reasoning. Experiences with rectangular arrays, the use of pictures, materials, and situations involving equal groups, and the language and notation of multiplication are also helpful and supportive to students' understanding. Rich experiences and games with many opportunities to share mathematical thinking over time will provide students with a firm foundation.

Many teachers have students begin their study of multiplication by memorizing the basic multiplication facts. However, when memorization is the initial and most important focus, students have little opportunity to develop conceptual understanding of multiplication. Rote practice and memorization provide little support for developing multiplicative reasoning skills.

To memorize all the facts from 0×0 to 9×9 requires learning one hundred pieces of information. That is a daunting task! A child who experiences multiplication as separate, unrelated bits of memorized information may know $6 \times 8 = 48$ yet fail to use this information to solve 8×6 by applying the commutative property of multiplication or fail to use the information to figure 7×8 by adding one more group of 8 to 48.

Teaching what multiplication means before asking children to memorize the multiplication facts simplifies the task of learning the multiplication tables. When children develop understanding prior to learning the basic multiplication facts, they can apply, for example, the commutative property of multiplication. This reduces the number of multiplication facts from one hundred to fifty-five! Understanding and applying the identity property of multiplication (multiplying by one) and understanding multiplication by zero reduces the number by another nineteen, leaving thirty-six facts to learn. Most students know the twos, or doubles, from their experiences in first and second grade, eliminating another eight facts, leaving twenty-eight facts. Many children easily skip-count by five and are familiar with the fives, which accounts for another seven facts. The student is left with twenty-one facts to learn, a far more reasonable feat, which can be accomplished through many experiences over time that develop understanding of multiplication. (See Figure 5–1.) When faced with an unknown fact, say 8×7,

0×0, 0×1, 0×2, 0×3, 0×4, 0×5, 0×6, 0×7, 0×8, 0×9

1×0, 1×1, 1×2, 1×3, 1×4, 1×5, 1×6, 1×7, 1×8, 1×9

2×0, 2×1, 2×2, 2×3, 2×4, 2×5, 2×6, 2×7, 2×8, 2×9

3×0, 3×1, 3×2, (3 × 3,) 3×4, 3×5, 3×6, 3×7, 3×8, 3×9

4×0, 4×1, 4×2, (4 × 3,) (4 × 4,) 4×5, 4×6, 4×7, 4×8, 4×9

5×0, 5×1, 5×2, 5×3, 5×4, 5×5, 5×6, 5×7, 5×8, 5×9

6×0, 6×1, 6×2, (6 × 3,) (6 × 4,) 6×5, (6 × 6,) 6×7, 6×8, 6×9

7×0, 7×1, 7×2, (7 × 3,) (7 × 4,) 7×5, (7 × 6,) (7 × 7,) 7×8, 7×9

8×0, 8×1, 8×2, (8 × 3,) (8 × 4,) 8×5, (8 × 6,) (8 × 7,) (8 × 8,) 8×9

9×0, 9×1, 9×2, (9 × 3,) (9 × 4,) 9×5, (9 × 6,) (9 × 7,) (9 × 8,) (9 × 9)

FIGURE 5–1   Facts remaining to be learned.

students with deep, well-developed understanding know that they can figure the answer by thinking $8 \times 7 = (4 \times 7) + (4 \times 7) = 28 + 28 = 56$; or $8 \times 7 = (8 \times 5) + (8 \times 2) = 40 + 16 = 56$; or $8 \times 7 = (7 \times 7) + 7 = 56$; or $8 \times 7 = 7 \times 8 = (8 \times 8) - 8 = 56$; and so on. Students need to develop fluency and accuracy with the basic multiplication facts. Teaching for understanding prior to asking students to memorize facts facilitates memorization and provides a strong foundation for future learning, such as learning the basic division facts, performing multiplication and division with larger numbers, working with fractions, and doing algebra.

Multiplication on Standardized Tests

Few test items are purely computational in nature, for example: $7 \times 9 = ?$ (And those few questions that are purely computational do not require a student to use one particular method to find the answer.) Rather, tests present students with a situation and, based on the information provided, the student must reason and apply her knowledge to make sense of the situation and find a solution in a reasonable amount of time. Students need to be able to think and reason in an efficient, accurate manner that allows them to make sense of the mathematics.

Following are some examples of how various states test basic understanding of multiplication. The state and standard addressed from each state's content standards are included:

What is one way to tell how many squares there are below?

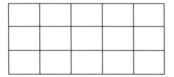

A. 3 + 5

B. 2 × 4

C. 3 × 5

(From Michigan Educational Assessment Program, grade 3, Fall 2006. N.MR.02.14: "Represent multiplication using area and array models.")

Which of the following is represented by the model below?

☆ ☆ ☆ ☆
☆ ☆ ☆ ☆
☆ ☆ ☆ ☆

A. 4 + 4

B. 3 × 4

C. 3 + 4

(From Michigan Educational Assessment Program, grade 3, Fall 2006. N.MR.02.14: "Represent multiplication using area and array models.")

Tina bought 3 boxes of crayons. Each box had 6 crayons. Which of the following can be used to determine the total number of crayons she bought?

A. 3 + 6 = ?

B. 3 − 6 = ?

(Continued on page 62.)

C. 3 ÷ 6 = ?

D. 3 × 6 = ?

(From Michigan Educational Assessment Program, grade 4, Fall 2006. N.MR.03.10: "Recognize multiplication and division situations.")

In these problems, no computation is necessary. Conceptual understanding is the key to the solution of each question. Providing students with many hands-on, problem-solving experiences with multiplication is time well spent. Activities such as *Circles and Stars* and *Exploring Candy Boxes,* from *Teaching Arithmetic: Lessons for Introducing Multiplication, Grade 3* (Burns 2001) and *About Teaching Mathematics: A K–8 Resource* (Burns 2007), support this learning. The key to all activities and games is asking a variety of carefully chosen questions to give students opportunities to make connections among different ideas related to multiplication. To further enhance learning, ask students to explain their thinking and strategies both orally in class discussions and in writing by using words, pictures, and numbers.

In addition to recognizing multiplication as equal groups and as rectangular arrays, students leaving third grade should be able to

- represent a multiplication situation by drawing a picture;
- explain that the times sign can be read as "groups of";
- explain how multiplication relates to repeated addition;
- explain how multiplication relates to skip-counting;
- apply the commutative property;
- explain that while 4 × 3 and 3 × 4 both equal 12, they represent two different situations;
- figure products up to 12 × 12;
- figure products for two- and three-digit numbers multiplied by one-digit numbers;
- solve real-world problems that involve multiplication; and
- relate multiplication to division.

This list, from Wickett and Burns (2001), is not necessarily hierarchical, but is intended to give you a sense of the kinds of understandings students should have. All of these ideas are included on state assessments in one form or another. Following are a few examples.

Apply the commutative property

Which number, when placed in the $\square$, makes the number sentence true?

$5 \times 16 = \square \times 5$

A. 1

B. 16

C. 50

D. 80

(From 2006 New Mexico Standards-Based Assessment, grade 3. Algebra
Standard 3.5: "Recognize and use the commutative property of multiplication.")

Children need to know two things to get this problem correct. First, they
must understand that the equals sign indicates that quantities on either side
are equivalent amounts. Those who don't understand this may pick D as the
right answer, interpreting the equals sign as an indicator to perform an operation rather than an indicator of a relationship. These children will figure the
answer to 5×16 to get 80. The second thing children need to know is the
commutative property of multiplication. The child who understands both of
these ideas will quickly choose B.

*Figure products for two- and three-digit numbers multiplied
by one-digit numbers*

Toni has 8 class periods in one school day. How many class periods does she
have in one school year if the school year is 180 days?

A. 188

B. 1,160

C. 1,440

D. 2,920

(From 2006 Michigan Educational Assessment Program, grade 5.
N.MR.04.14: "Solve problems involving multiplication and
division.")

Children who lack multiplicative reasoning skills typically select A
because they add the two numbers involved. Those who can apply

multiplicative reasoning skills will understand that they can find the solution by using repeated addition. The use of repeated addition is evidence of emerging multiplicative reasoning; the student knows that one of the numbers represents the number of groups, or sets, of the other number.

Solve real-world problems that involve multiplication

The table below shows some magazine subscription prices for 1, 2, or 3 years.

Years	Price
1	$35.00
2	$70.00
3	$105.00

If the price stays the same, what is the subscription price for 4 years?

A. $135.00

B. $140.00

C. $175.00

D. $210.00

(From Fall 2006 Michigan Educational Assessment Program, grade 4.)

There are several ways students can successfully solve this problem. One way is to recognize that the number in the left-hand column when multiplied by thirty-five generates the number in the right-hand column. To solve the problem, one can multiply four times thirty-five. Another approach is to recognize that on the left side of the chart, the numbers increase by one as you move down the chart. On the right side of the chart, the numbers increase by thirty-five as you move down the chart. A student could solve the problem by adding thirty-five to one hundred five. Either way, the answer is $140.00, and in both cases, mathematical reasoning and understanding are required.

Relate multiplication to division
Students who understand the inverse nature of multiplication and division will efficiently and accurately use their understanding to solve problems. (See Figure 5–2.)

26 The figure below is a model for the multiplication sentence.

$$8 \times 4 = 32$$

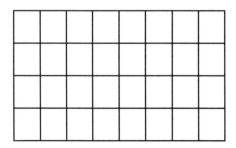

Which division sentence is modeled by the same figure?

A $8 \div 4 = 2$

B $12 \div 4 = 3$

C $24 \div 8 = 3$

D $32 \div 8 = 4$

CSM01096

27 Lily did this division problem.

$$375 \div 25 = 15$$

Which problem could she do to check her answer?

A $25 + 15 = \square$

B $25 - 15 = \square$

C $25 \times 15 = \square$

D $25 \div 15 = \square$

CSM01040

FIGURE 5–2 Two of California's 2007 Grade 3 released test items for Standard 3NS2.3: "Use the inverse relationship of multiplication and division to compute and check results."

Other types of multiplication problems

Besides problems involving equal grouping and rectangular arrays, there are other types of multiplication problems, which should be included in children's study of multiplication as well.

- *Rate problems:* An example of a rate problem is figuring the cost of amusement park tickets for four people if each ticket costs $18.

- *Multiplicative compare problems:* An example of a multiplicative compare problem is figuring the number of miles James ran this week if last week he ran 6 miles and this week he ran four times as many miles as last week.

- *Cartesian product problems:* An example of a Cartesian product problem follows:

  Sarita bought two skirts and four shirts. How many outfits can she make from her skirts and shirts?

Examples of these problem types can be found on many state tests. The following example is a released question from Florida's 2000 sample grade 4 test:

Pat is making a key ring by stringing beads on a leather strip. He may choose one of the following 2 colors for the leather strip.

BLACK   WHITE

Then he may choose one of the following 3 colors for the beads.

RED   BLUE   YELLOW

How many different color combinations can Pat make?

A. 8

B. 6

C. 4

D. 2

Different states have different time lines, methods, and purposes for testing basic multiplication concepts. For this reason it is important to check your state's standards and sample and released test items to learn when and how these skills will be assessed.

Extending Multiplication

Students with a firm understanding of the concept of multiplication as just described, along with a strong understanding of place value and the base ten number system, are ready to learn how to

- multiply by ten, powers of ten, and multiples of ten; and

- use the distributive property to accurately and efficiently calculate products both with paper and pencil and mentally.

Students who expect mathematics in general, and multiplication in particular, to make sense will quickly discover patterns that occur when multiplying a number by ten, powers of ten, and multiples of ten. Games and investigations along with class discussions are good ways to help students discover these patterns for themselves. The games *Target 300* and *Times 10*, from Wickett and Burns (2001), and *Race to 200, Multiplication by Ten and One Hundred*, and *What's My Rule?* from Wickett and Burns (2005), are useful for helping students make sense of the patterns. *Related Rectangles, True or False: 30 × 6 = 6 × 3 × 10*, and *True or False: 400 × 8 = 8 × 4 × 100*, also from Wickett and Burns (2001), develop understanding of how to use the distributive property.

An Alternative Algorithm

There are different algorithms used throughout the world to solve multiplication problems involving larger numbers. The algorithm typically taught in the United States is not necessarily taught internationally. While it is an efficient method, there are problems with the algorithm many of us learned and that many of our students are taught today. For example, as a result of trying to memorize a poorly understood procedure, students give up their right to make sense of a problem and end up discarding their knowledge of number sense. This occurs in part because the place value represented by each digit is discounted and all digits are treated as if they were ones. An often confusing system of placeholders is used as a result of treating each digit as if it were in the ones place. When students abandon sense making, they have little to fall back on to check if their results are reasonable for the situation.

For a fuller discussion of the alternative algorithms for multiplying large numbers, take a look at *Math Matters* (Chapin and Johnson 2006). The alternative algorithm presented here is often referred to as the *partial product method* and is found in a few math textbooks. We include this method because it encourages sense making and keeps students' number sense intact. Prerequisite skills for this algorithm include:

- fluency with basic multiplication facts
- skill with addition
- skill with multiplying by ten and multiples of ten
- skill with decomposing numbers and place value
- skill with multiplying by powers of ten

There are three basic steps for applying the partial product algorithm:

1. Decompose the factors.
2. Multiply to find the partial products.
3. Add the partial products to find the final product.

The partial product algorithm was used to solve the following problems:

$15 \times 3 =$

$15 = 10 + 5$

$$\begin{array}{r} \times\ 3 \\ \hline 3 \times\ 5 = 15 \\ 3 \times 10 = 30 \\ \hline 45 \end{array}$$

$265 \times 4 =$

$265 = 200 + 60 + 5$

$$\begin{array}{r} \times\ 4 \\ \hline 4 \times\ \ 5 = \ \ 20 \\ 4 \times\ 60 = 240 \\ 4 \times 200 = 800 \\ \hline 1{,}060 \end{array}$$

$4{,}159 \times 6 =$

$4{,}159 = 4{,}000 + 100 + 50 + 9$

$$\begin{array}{r} \times\ \ \ \ \ 6 \\ \hline 6 \times 9 = \ \ \ \ 54 \\ 6 \times 50 = \ \ \ 300 \\ 6 \times 100 = \ \ \ 600 \\ 6 \times 4{,}000 = 2{,}400 \\ \hline 3{,}354 \end{array}$$

$53 \times 14 =$

$53 = 50 + 3$

$14 = 10 + 4$

$$\begin{array}{r} \hline 4 \times 3 = \ \ 12 \\ 4 \times 50 = 200 \\ 10 \times 3 = \ \ 30 \\ 10 \times 50 = 500 \\ \hline 742 \end{array}$$

$$356 \times 24 =$$
$$356 = 300 + 50 + 6$$
$$24 = 20 + 4$$
$$\overline{}$$
$$4 \times 6 = 24$$
$$4 \times 50 = 200$$
$$4 \times 300 = 1{,}200$$
$$20 \times 6 = 120$$
$$20 \times 50 = 1{,}000$$
$$20 \times 300 = 6{,}000$$
$$\overline{}$$
$$8{,}544$$

The following test item can be solved with this algorithm. Many states have similar items on their fourth- or fifth-grade tests. Many state content standards include using the distributive property to solve multiplication problems.

Which expression is equal to 4×87?

A. $(4 \times 8) + (4 \times 7)$

B. $(4 + 80) \times (4 \times 7)$

C. $(4 \times 80) + (4 \times 7)$

D. $(4 + 80) + (4 + 7)$

*(From 2006 Michigan Educational Assessment Program, grade 5.
N.ME.04.09: "Solve multiplication problems using the distributive property.")*

The Illinois Standards Achievement Test has asked a similar question:

Which number sentence is true?

A. $15 \times 3 = (10 \times 3) \div (5 \times 3)$

B. $15 \times 3 = (10 \times 3) \times (5 \times 3)$

C. $15 \times 3 = (10 \times 3) - (5 \times 3)$

D. $15 \times 3 = (10 \times 3) + (5 \times 3)$

*(From 2008 Illinois Standards Achievement Test, Mathematics Samples,
grade 4. 6.4.14: "Solve problems involving the commutative and
distributive properties of operations on whole numbers.")*

---

28 There are 40 teachers at a school. Each
teacher is provided with 2500 sheets of paper.
How many sheets of paper is this in all?

    A   10,000

    B   100,000

    C   1,000,000

    D   10,000,000

CSM01129

FIGURE 5–3   One of California's 2004 Grade 4 released test items for Standard
4NS3.3: "Solve problems involving multiplication of multi-digit numbers by two-digit numbers."

An example from California involves multiplication with multiples of
ten and multiples of one hundred. Number sense is challenged by the magnitude of the numbers involved. (See Figure 5–3.)

The partial product algorithm provides an accurate and efficient
method for solving test examples. (See Figure 5–4 and the following test
items from Florida and Arizona.)

In the United States, about 350 slices of pizza per second are eaten
by pizza lovers. About how many slices of pizza are eaten in
one minute?

1 minute = 60 seconds

F. 2,100

G. 8,400

H. 18,000

I. 21,000

(From 2005 Florida released test items, grade 4. MA.A.3.2.3: "The
student solves real-world problems involving addition, subtraction,
multiplication, and division of whole numbers.")

29 A year has 365 days, and a day has 24 hours. How many hours are in 365 days?

A   2190

B   7440

C   7679

D   8760

CSM21080

FIGURE 5–4   One of California's 2006 Grade 4 released test items for Standard 4NS3.3: "Solve problems involving multiplication of multi-digit numbers by two-digit numbers."

Mr. Veno's class of 17 students collected canned goods for charity. Each student collected 29 cans. What was the total number of cans collected?

A. 46

B. 232

C. 333

D. 493

(From 2005 Arizona's Instruments to Measure Standards, grade 5. Concept PO2: "Solve word problems using grade-level appropriate operations and numbers.")

All of these examples can be solved efficiently and accurately using the partial product algorithm.

Advantages to a Problem-Solving Approach to Multiplication

There are several important advantages to using the partial product approach:

- It builds on prior knowledge (basic facts, place value, decomposing, addition) and provides a foundation for future learning.

- It teaches for understanding so students retain the information and are able to apply it to both familiar and new situations.

- It greatly reduces the need for reteaching because students understand it.

- It reduces the many errors students make when using zero as a placeholder.

- When students do make errors, their answers are still reasonable and they are more likely to catch their errors.

- It builds on and incorporates number sense.

- It gives students tools to estimate answers and check for reasonableness of answers.

- It is an efficient, accurate algorithm applicable to test taking and future learning.

Resources

Following are some additional resources to help you think more about multiplicative thinking, alternative algorithms, and lessons that support teaching for understanding:

Burns, Marilyn. 2001. *Teaching Arithmetic: Lessons for Introducing Multiplication, Grade 3.* Sausalito, CA: Math Solutions.

———. 2007. *About Teaching Mathematics: A K–8 Resource.* 3d ed. Sausalito, CA: Math Solutions.

Chapin, Suzanne, and Art Johnson. 2006. *Math Matters: Understanding the Math You Teach, Grades K–8.* 2d ed. Sausalito, CA: Math Solutions.

Fosnot, Catherine Twomey, and Maarten Dolk. 2001. *Young Mathematicians at Work: Constructing Multiplication and Division.* Portsmouth, NH: Heinemann.

Van de Walle, John. 2006. *Elementary and Middle School Mathematics: Teaching Developmentally.* 6th ed. Boston: Allyn and Bacon.

Wickett, Maryann, and Marilyn Burns. 2001. *Teaching Arithmetic: Lessons for Extending Multiplication, Grades 4–5.* Sausalito, CA: Math Solutions.

———. 2005. *Teaching Arithmetic: Lessons for Extending Place Value, Grade 3.* Sausalito, CA: Math Solutions.

Chapter 6

Teaching and Testing Division

A long-standing right of passage for upper-elementary students is the study of division. This often daunting task doesn't need to be so. When students have a strong understanding and working knowledge of multiplication, place value, and subtraction, division makes sense and becomes an extension of their prior knowledge. Linking multiplication and division is a powerful way to access, explore, and come to understand division. Children who believe math makes sense and apply their prior understandings have a powerful foundation for success with division. One way to link multiplication to division is to help children discover and understand that the two are inverse operations, that is, $3 \times 4 = 12$ is the inverse of $12 \div 4 = 3$. When children understand the basic concept of multiplication, the connections among the basic multiplication facts, as discussed in Chapter 5, and the inverse relationship between multiplication and division, they already have a significant amount of knowledge and understanding about division.

Both multiplication and division are multiplicative and are about equal groups. What distinguishes division from multiplication is what is known and what is unknown. In multiplication situations, the number of groups and the number in each group are known. The unknown is the total number. In division, the total is known and either the number of groups or the amount in each group is unknown.

Two Models of Division

There are two models of division. The context of a problem determines which model is used based on what is known and what is unknown. In all division problems the total number is known: it's the dividend. Also known is one of the following: the number of groups *or* the number in each group. In either case, this is the divisor.

In one division model, called the sharing, or partitive, model, the unknown is the number in each group. Here's an example of this situation:

> *Carlos has 12 toy cars. He wants to split them evenly among 4 friends. How many toy cars will each friend get?*

A specific number of items, the total, is shared equally among a known number of groups, the friends. The unknown is how many in each group, or how many cars each gets.

In the second model, called the grouping, or quotative, model, the unknown is the number of groups. For example:

> *Carlos has 12 toy cars. He wants to put them into groups of 4. How many groups can he make?*

While both models can be represented with the same equation, the resulting pictures along with the underlying thinking and approaches to solving the problems are different.

Sharing, or partitive, context

> *Carlos has 12 toy cars. He wants to split them equally among 4 friends. How many cars will each friend get?*

The equation is $12 \div 4 = 3$, meaning twelve cars divided equally among four friends equals three cars for each friend.

To solve this problem by drawing a picture, the student may first draw four circles or children to represent the four groups. Then most students will draw one representation of a car in the first group, then one in the second group, one in the third group, and one in the fourth group, and repeat this divvying-up process until all twelve cars have been distributed equally among the friends:

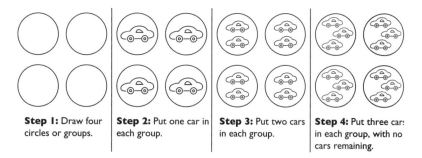

Step 1: Draw four circles or groups.

Step 2: Put one car in each group.

Step 3: Put two cars in each group.

Step 4: Put three cars in each group, with no cars remaining.

Grouping, or quotative, context

Carlos has 12 toy cars. He wants to put them into groups of 4. How many groups can he make?

Again, the equation is 12 ÷ 4 = 3, but this time it means that twelve cars are divided equally into groups of four, resulting in three groups of four.

To solve this problem, students will frequently begin by first drawing a group of four cars, followed by another group of four cars, followed by the third and final group of four cars:

Step 1: Draw one group of four cars.

Step 2: Draw a second group of four cars.

Step 3: Draw a third and last group of four cars, with no cars remaining.

When children are initially introduced to division, they are often presented with the sharing model of division. An example is sharing twelve cookies between two children, a situation explored in *The Doorbell Rang* (Hutchins 1994), a book commonly used to introduce children to division. Sharing is a real-life situation that all children know well.

It is important to expand children's experiences with division to include grouping problems. It is the grouping model that is generally used to solve long-division problems. Consider the following problem: 164 ÷ 7. The first thing we ask is, "How many groups of seven in one hundred sixty-four?" This is the grouping model. If children experience division only as sharing, they are often confused by a problem like this.

Division on Standardized Tests

Following are some test items that target basic division skills. Understanding the concept of division plays an important role in answering all of these test questions. The first three items require no computation, only understanding of the concept of division.

The first item involves fact families and the relationship between multiplication and division:

Which number goes in the box to complete the following fact family?

$$4 \times 8 = 32$$

$$8 \times 4 = 32$$

$$32 \div 8 = 4$$

$$32 \div 4 = \square$$

> *A. 9*
>
> *B. 8*
>
> *C. 7*
>
> *D. 6*

(From 2006 Michigan Educational Assessment Program, grade 4. N.MR.03.09: "Use multiplication and division to show the inverse relationship.")

The next two items (see Figure 6–1 and the following page) require the student to be able to recognize and represent numerically a situation involving division.

---

40 **Mr. Guzman bought 48 doughnuts packed equally into 4 boxes. Which number sentence shows how to find the number of doughnuts in each box?**

A $48 - 4 = \square$

B $48 \div 4 = \square$

C $48 + 4 = \square$

D $48 \times 4 = \square$

CSM02176

FIGURE 6–1   One of California's 2003 Grade 3 released test items for Standard 3AF1.1 "Represent relationships of quantities in the form of mathematical expressions, equations, or inequalities."

There are 20 people at a family party. Each family has 4 people. Which of the following can be used to find the number of families at the party?

A. 20 + 4

B. 20 × 4

C. 20 − 4

D. 20 ÷ 4

(From 2006 Michigan Educational Assessment Program, grade 4. N.MR.03.10: "Recognize multiplication and division situations.")

The next two examples (see below and Figure 6–2) require knowledge of basic facts:

Which mathematics fact has a value different from the others?

A. 15 ÷ 3

B. 25 ÷ 5

C. 1 × 5

D. 10 ÷ 5

(From 2006 Michigan Educational Assessment Program, grade 4. N.FL.03.11: "Find products to 10 × 10 and related quotients.")

---

47 **Which sign goes in the box to make the number sentence true?**

$$48 \ \square \ 6 = 8$$

A +

B −

C ×

D ÷

CSM01071

FIGURE 6–2   One of California's 2004 Grade 3 released test items for Standard 3AF1.3 "Select appropriate operational and relational symbols to make an expression true."

The following three test items require the student to understand a word problem and compute the answer. The item shown in Figure 6–3 is another example of the sharing model. The item from Illinois, below, and the one from Florida, at the top of the next page, are grouping, or quotative, problems:

The average length of a song on a CD is 3 minutes. Which is closest to the number of songs that can be played in 16 minutes?

A. 19

B. 13

C. 5

D. 3

(From 2008 Illinois Standards Achievement Test Mathematics Samples, grade 4. 6.4.16: "Make estimates appropriate to a given situation with whole numbers.")

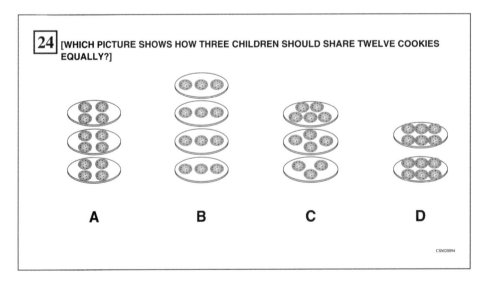

FIGURE 6–3   One of California's 2005 Grade 2 released test items for Standard 2NS3.2 "Use repeated subtraction, equal sharing, and forming equal groups with remainders to do division."

Carl Fabergé created fancy eggs for the rulers of Russia. A museum plans to show some of the eggs. The eggs will be shown in glass cases. Each case will hold 3 eggs. If 27 eggs are being shown, how many glass cases will be needed?

A. 3

B. 9

C. 27

D. 30

(From 2006 Florida Comprehensive Assessment Test, grade 3. MA.3A.1.1: "Model multiplication and division including problems presented in context, repeated addition, multiplicative comparison, array, how many combinations, measurement, partitioning.")

To develop a full understanding of division, students need many experiences over time with division situations with and without remainders. Students often don't understand what a remainder represents. Consider the following problem:

Jordan has 11 marbles. She wants to split the marbles equally among 5 bags. How many will be in each bag?

The answer could be 2 R1, $2\frac{1}{5}$, or 2.2. What does the R1 represent in the first solution? Does it mean one bag? One marble? One what? In this case, it means that there will be one marble remaining. Which of these answers is appropriate to the situation? The answer with the remainder is most appropriate, given that marbles cannot be split into fifths or tenths. Students who understand a division situation can make sense of a remainder within the context of the problem.

Consider this similar problem:

Jordan has 11 cookies and she wants to split them equally into 5 groups. How many will be in each group?

Again, the answer could be 2 R1 or $2\frac{1}{5}$ or 2.2. A student who makes sense of mathematical situations will see that all the answers are appropriate because the final cookie could remain whole (R1), or it could be split into five equal parts, with each group getting one part ($\frac{1}{5}$), or it could be split into ten equal parts, with each group getting two parts (.2).

Following is an example of how Michigan tests its fourth graders' understanding of remainders:

Marco has 16 slices of apple to share equally among himself and 2 friends. He knows that 16 ÷ 3 = 5 R1. What does R1 represent?

A. the number of apples slices left over after each person gets an equal amount

B. the greatest number of apple slices Marco can give to each person

C. the number of people to whom Marco gives apples slices

D. the total number of apple slices Marco has to share

(From 2006 Michigan Standard N.MR.03.14: "Solve division problems involving remainders.")

In addition to having many experiences with thinking about remainders in context, students also need to be exposed to all three forms of representing division. Sometimes division problems should be represented with the division sign (÷), sometimes with the division bracket ($\overline{)}$), and sometimes as a fraction. For example:

$$49 \div 7 \qquad 7\overline{)49} \qquad \frac{49}{7}$$

Students leaving third grade should be able to

- explain that division involves equal groups;

- recognize the two types of division problems—sharing (partitioning) and grouping (quotative)—and be able to think flexibly about both;

- represent remainders in different ways, choosing a representation that is appropriate within the context of the problem;

- represent division problems symbolically in three different ways: $12 \div 4 = 3, 4\overline{)12}^{\,3}$, and $\frac{12}{4} = 3$;

- figure quotients up to $144 \div 12$;

- interpret division in real-world situations;

- solve problems that involve division; and

- explain how division relates to multiplication. (Wickett and Burns 2003, x)

Extending Division

Students in the fourth and fifth grades should be able to build on their understanding of place value and the base ten number system along with their skill in multiplying by ten, multiples of ten, and powers of ten to learn how to

- calculate problems with up to two-digit divisors and three- and four-digit dividends accurately and efficiently; and
- explain how division relates to subtraction and multiplication.

An Alternative Algorithm

The alternative algorithm presented here can be found in some math textbooks. It is often referred to as the partial quotient method. As you will see, this algorithm relies heavily on multiplication by ten, multiples of ten, and powers of ten. Prerequisite skills for this algorithm include:

- fluency with basic subtraction, multiplication, and division facts
- skill with subtraction and addition
- skill with multiplying by ten, multiples of ten, and powers of ten
- number sense
- understanding of remainders and how to represent them meaningfully

Often when students are presented with the standard U.S. algorithm for division, they practice the procedure one step at a time, making little sense of what they are trying to do or what the numbers represent. They divide, multiply, subtract, and bring down, repeating these steps as necessary until the remainder is less than the divisor. Students are often taught to memorize these steps by thinking of their family: Dad, Mom, Sister, Brother. In this memorized routine, the numbers in the dividend are treated as if all were in the ones place. There is no acknowledgment of tens, hundreds, thousands, and so on. Students have no opportunity to make sense of what they are doing. Another confusing oddity of this algorithm is that the process begins with the left side of the dividend, and students who have learned the other standard algorithms have consistently started with the right side, or the ones place.

Up to this point in their study of division, students may have had experience only with the sharing model of division. They have thought of division only as "How many in each group?" or "How many will each person get?" Long division asks a different question: "How many groups of . . . ?" Children need experiences with both models of division so they won't be confused by different questions. Because students lose their number sense when using the standard algorithm, they make mistakes when zero is involved in the quotient and come up with absurd answers without recognizing the absurdity.

Because it is unlikely that students will be tested on the process of the standard division algorithm, consider teaching other methods. The alternative algorithm presented here is efficient and accurate, builds on previous knowledge of place value, eliminates difficulties with zero in the quotient, and promotes understanding and number sense.

An important aspect of the partial quotient algorithm is that it takes into account the entire value of the dividend, instead of treating each digit as if it were in the ones place. Students who can multiply by ones, tens, multiples of ten, and powers of ten will be successful with this approach. It is important to help students link their knowledge of multiplication by ones, tens, multiples of ten, and powers of ten to division and see how this knowledge is useful. They can begin the division process by considering whether or not there are ten groups of the divisor, for example, in the dividend. There are five steps to this algorithm:

1. Divide.
2. Multiply.
3. Subtract.
4. Repeat Steps 1 through 3 until the remainder is less than the divisor.
5. Add the partial quotients.

Let's look at the problem $48 \div 4 =$ _____. To begin Step 1, guide students to consider the divisor and the dividend. Help students make use of their number sense and ability to multiply by one, ten, one hundred, and so on. For example, ask students, "Are there ten fours [the divisor] in forty-eight [the dividend]?" The answer is yes. Step 2 is multiply, so multiply 10×4 to find how many of the 48 are used in the division. Record as follows:

$$
\begin{array}{r}
10 \\
4 \overline{\smash{)}48}
\end{array}
$$
$$10 \times 4 = 40$$

For Step 3, subtract to find how many remain to be divided:

$$
\begin{array}{r}
10 \\
4 \overline{\smash{)}48}
\end{array}
$$
$$
\begin{array}{r}
10 \times 4 = 40 \\
\underline{8}
\end{array}
$$

Step 4 states to repeat Steps 1 through 3 until the remainder is less than the divisor. Eight remain and eight is more than four, so we must repeat Steps 1 through 3. Going back to Step 1, ask students, "Are there ten fours in eight?" The answer is no. Ask students, "Are there five fours in eight?" Again the answer is no. Ask, "Are there two fours in eight?" The answer is yes. Follow Steps 2 and 3, record the multiplication, and subtract to find the number remaining. Ask students, "Are there any groups of four in zero?" The answer is no. Add the partial quotients to find the answer: $2 + 10 = 12$.

$$
\begin{array}{r}
2 \\
10 \\
\end{array} \Big\rangle 12
$$

$$
\begin{array}{r}
4 \overline{)48} \\
10 \times 4 = 40 \\
\hline
8 \\
2 \times 4 = 8 \\
\hline
0 \\
\end{array}
$$

Now let's look at $38 \div 4 = \underline{\hspace{1cm}}$. This problem is more challenging because it involves a remainder. However, the steps and questions are the same. Before reading further, you might want to try the process yourself. The initial question is "Are there ten fours in thirty-eight?" The answer is no. Ask, "Are there five fours in thirty-eight?" The answer is yes. Multiply 5×4 to find how many of the 38 are used in the division. Record as follows:

$$
\begin{array}{r}
5 \\
4 \overline{)38} \\
5 \times 4 = 20 \\
\end{array}
$$

Now subtract to find how many remain to be divided:

$$
\begin{array}{r}
5 \\
4 \overline{)38} \\
5 \times 4 = 20 \\
\hline
18 \\
\end{array}
$$

Ask, "Are there five fours in eighteen?" The answer is no. Ask, "Are there four fours in eighteen?" The answer is yes. Record the multiplication and subtract to find the number remaining.

$$
\begin{array}{r}
4 \\
5 \\
4\,\overline{)38} \\
5 \times 4 = \underline{20} \\
18 \\
4 \times 4 = \underline{16} \\
2
\end{array}
$$

Ask, "Are there any groups of four in two?" The answer is no. Add the partial quotients to find the answer: $4 + 5 = 9$ with a remainder of 2. The answer is 9 R2. Depending on the context, the answer could result in a fraction or decimal, in this case, $9\frac{1}{2}$ or 9.5.

An important aspect of this algorithm is that there are many entry points. A student could have taken out one group of four nine times rather than a group of five fours followed by a group of four fours. Or a student could have taken out nine groups of four. Because of this flexibility, students can solve the problem in a variety of ways, giving access to everyone with the prerequisite skills.

Let's consider $78 \div 5 = $ _____. This problem involves slightly larger numbers. Again, you may want to try it yourself before reading further. The steps and questions are the same. The initial question is "Are there ten fives in seventy-eight?" The answer is yes. Multiply 10×5 to find how many of the 78 are used in the division. Record as follows:

$$
\begin{array}{r}
10 \\
5\,\overline{)78} \\
10 \times 5 = 50
\end{array}
$$

Now subtract to find how many remain to be divided.

$$
\begin{array}{r}
10 \\
5\,\overline{)78} \\
10 \times 5 = \underline{50} \\
28
\end{array}
$$

Ask, "Are there ten fives in twenty-eight?" The answer is no. Ask, "Are there five fives in twenty-eight?" The answer is yes. Record the multiplication and subtract to find the number remaining.

$$
\begin{array}{r}
5 \\
10 \\
\end{array} \!\!> 15\ R3
$$

$$
5\,\overline{)78}
$$

$$
\begin{array}{r}
10 \times 5 = 50 \\
\hline
28 \\
5 \times 5 = 25 \\
\hline
3
\end{array}
$$

Ask, "Are there any groups of five in three?" The answer is no. Add the partial quotients to find the answer: $10 + 5 = 15$ with a remainder of 3. Depending on the context, the answer could be a fraction or decimal, in this case, $15\frac{3}{5}$ or 15.6.

Following are some other ways students might solve this and other problems. Try the problems yourself first. There are many ways to solve each problem using the partial quotient method.

$78 \div 5 =$	$78 \div 5 =$
$\begin{array}{r} 5 \\ 5 \\ 5 \end{array}\!\!> 15\ R3$ $5\,\overline{)78}$ $5 \times 5 = 25$ $\overline{53}$ $5 \times 5 = 25$ $\overline{28}$ $5 \times 5 = 25$ $\overline{3}$	$\begin{array}{r} 10 \\ 5 \end{array}\!\!> 15\ R3$ $5\,\overline{)78}$ $5 \times 5 = 25$ $\overline{53}$ $10 \times 5 = 50$ $\overline{3}$

78 ÷ 5 =

$$
\begin{array}{r}
1 \\
1 \\
1 \\
1 \\
1 \\
10 \\
\end{array}
\Bigg] \quad 15\ R3
$$

$$
5 \ \overline{)\,78}
$$

$10 \times 5 = \dfrac{50}{}$
$\quad\quad 28$

$1 \times 5 = \dfrac{5}{}$
$\quad\quad 23$

$1 \times 5 = \dfrac{5}{}$
$\quad\quad 18$

$1 \times 5 = \dfrac{5}{}$
$\quad\quad 13$

$1 \times 5 = \dfrac{5}{}$
$\quad\quad 8$

$1 \times 5 = \dfrac{5}{}$
$\quad\quad 3$

140 ÷ 5 =

$$
\begin{array}{r}
4 \\
4 \\
10 \\
10 \\
\end{array}
\Bigg\rangle\ 28
$$

$$
5 \ \overline{)\,140}
$$

$10 \times 5 = \dfrac{50}{}$
$\quad\quad 90$

$10 \times 5 = \dfrac{50}{}$
$\quad\quad 40$

$4 \times 5 = \dfrac{20}{}$
$\quad\quad 20$

$4 \times 5 = \dfrac{20}{}$
$\quad\quad 0$

---

140 ÷ 5 =

$$
\begin{array}{r}
8 \\
20 \\
\end{array}
\Bigg\rangle\ 28
$$

$$
5 \ \overline{)\,140}
$$

$20 \times 5 = \dfrac{100}{}$
$\quad\quad 40$

$8 \times 5 = \dfrac{40}{}$
$\quad\quad 0$

251 ÷ 12 =

$$
\begin{array}{r}
10 \\
10 \\
\end{array}
\Bigg\rangle\ 20\ R11
$$

$$
12 \ \overline{)\,251}
$$

$10 \times 12 = \dfrac{120}{}$
$\quad\quad 131$

$10 \times 12 = \dfrac{120}{}$
$\quad\quad 11$

$4,614 \div 45 =$

$$\begin{array}{r} 2 \\ 100 \end{array} \Big\rangle\ 102\ R24$$

$$45\ \overline{)4,614}$$
$$100 \times 45 = \underline{4,500}$$
$$114$$
$$2 \times 45 = \underline{\ \ 90}$$
$$24$$

$7,369 \div 35 =$

$$\begin{array}{r} 10 \\ 200 \end{array} \Big\rangle\ 210\ R19$$

$$35\ \overline{)7,369}$$
$$200 \times 35 = \underline{7,000}$$
$$369$$
$$10 \times 35 = \underline{\ \ 350}$$
$$19$$

Advantages to a Problem-Solving Approach to Division

There are several important advantages to using the partial quotient algorithm, as it

- builds on prior knowledge (basic facts, place value, subtraction, multiplication);

- provides multiple access points, enabling students with different skill levels to solve the problem accurately and efficiently;

- teaches for understanding so students retain the information, reducing the need for reteaching, and so students are able to apply their learning to both familiar and new situations;

- reduces the number of errors students make, and results in more reasonable mistakes when they do occur;

- enables students to catch their errors because their sense making and number sense are intact;

- has similarities to the standard algorithm and supports eventual transition to the standard algorithm;

- builds on and incorporates number sense;

- develops estimation and mental math skills; and

- transfers to the test-taking situation.

Resources

Following are additional resources to help you think more about alternative algorithms and lessons to support teaching for understanding:

Burns, Marilyn. 2007. *About Teaching Mathematics: A K–8 Resource.* 3d ed. Sausalito, CA: Math Solutions.

Chapin, Suzanne, and Art Johnson. 2006. *Math Matters: Understanding the Math You Teach, Grades K–8.* 2d ed. Sausalito, CA: Math Solutions.

Fosnot, Catherine Twomey, and Maarten Dolk. 2001. *Young Mathematicians at Work: Constructing Multiplication and Division.* Portsmouth, NH: Heinemann.

Hutchins, Pat. 1994. *The Doorbell Rang.* New York: Greenwillow Books.

Van de Walle, John. 2006. *Elementary and Middle School Mathematics: Teaching Developmentally.* 6th ed. Boston: Allyn and Bacon.

Wickett, Maryann, and Marilyn Burns. 2003. *Teaching Arithmetic: Lessons for Extending Division, Grades 4–5.* Sausalito, CA: Math Solutions.

Wickett, Maryann, Susan Ohanian, and Marilyn Burns. 2002. *Teaching Arithmetic: Lessons for Introducing Division, Grades 3–4.* Sausalito, CA: Math Solutions.

III

Developing an
Environment for Success

Success in school math requires a rigorous and well-designed instructional program that offers students many chances to develop mathematical understanding. Success in math, as in almost any school endeavor, is also dependent upon the learner's thoughts and feelings about her ability to do well. The next few chapters take a look at how teachers can provide social and emotional support to students as they develop as learners and test takers.

We first consider some possible ways to create a predisposition for learning among students, starting from the beginning of the school year. In Chapter 7 we focus on the importance of developing a caring community in your classroom, one that gives all students the message that they can and will learn.

We then look at some of the issues that are likely to arise as the testing period draws closer. The issues in Chapter 8 run the gamut from test anxiety to test-taking preparation. We also offer suggestions for keeping both the testing period and the aftermath of testing as positive as possible.

And finally, in Chapter 9, we explore how teachers can help parents and administrators understand the choices teachers have made regarding the math program and assessment, and also how to build positive bridges with these other important members of the school community so that students and teachers have the best chance for success.

Creating a positive learning environment requires thought and planning and can be very demanding. But the work ultimately pays off—at least tenfold for students and teachers alike—in the form of classrooms that are alive with learning.

Chapter 7

Creating a Classroom Culture That Supports Good Thinking and Good Testing

At the beginning of the school year, one of the most important tasks is to create a classroom culture in which your students feel safe, comfortable, and productive as learners. There are several aspects to consider when creating such an environment:

- the role of effort and persistence in success;
- the belief that students can and will make sense of mathematics;
- the importance of encouraging and honoring risk taking;
- communication and discussion;
- partner work; and
- mathematical tools.

Taking the time to build a caring community in your classroom will support the intellectual growth of all your students throughout the year. The intellectual growth students make, the confidence they gain, and the good mathematical thinking they do will provide the best opportunity for them to do well in school, in life, and on standardized testing.

The Role of Effort and Persistence

Effort and persistence seem to be the most important characteristics a successful learner can possess. Without these attributes, little learning or sense making is possible. Studies such as those reported by Marzano, Pickering, and Pollock (2001) indicate some students are unaware of the direct effect their efforts have on their achievement. It's important, then, that we teach our students explicitly about the connection between effort and achievement. We can do this by pointing out to them in specific ways how their success is directly related to their effort and persistence. For example, imagine that you observe a student get stuck using one approach and then try a second approach that leads to a successful outcome. Upon completion of the task, or as soon as possible, tell the student what you observed. Point out that making the best effort possible by persisting and trying the second approach led to the successful outcome. Another strategy is to share with students a personal story about a time when your efforts had a direct link to your success. It is also useful to share stories of how effort and persistence played a role in the success of well-known athletes, doctors, inventors, explorers, and social leaders. There are many examples in children's literature of the link between persistence and success that can be shared with children as read-alouds. Although we all live in a culture of instant gratification, children can and should learn to make their best effort and press on until their learning makes sense. Children who use persistence as a routine approach to all they do adopt a valuable skill that will serve them throughout their lives.

Carefully choosing developmentally appropriate mathematical tasks for your students to grapple with and explore is important to making the link between effort and success. Activities that are too hard will frustrate and discourage children while those that are too easy will provide no challenge or opportunity to persist. Activities that make good choices are those that

- have multiple solutions and access points;
- build on and extend previous learning; and
- are intriguing and challenging but not overwhelming.

Tasks such as these convey to students that their effort and persistence pay off and that learning makes sense and is useful. They will believe in themselves as learners and be eager to take on new challenges, including those confronting them on standardized tests.

There will be times when children persist and don't successfully complete a problem or find a solution. This, too, is a valuable lesson for them. We are not always successful in our efforts as human beings, but if we are observant and open, we can learn and benefit from every attempt we make. It is important to value students' efforts so that they get the idea that sometimes the journey is as valuable and meaningful as the destination. Again, it's helpful to share personal stories about yourself, or relate others' anecdotes, of times that best effort and persistence didn't immediately yield the desired results. An example of this is Thomas Edison's efforts with the lightbulb. It took thousands of failures before he was able to invent a filament that glowed for an extended period of time, thus giving us the lightbulb. Another example: after 2,500 years there are still mathematicians working on computing pi, already figured to more than one billion places!

The Belief That Students Can and Will Make Sense of Math

Frank Smith states, "The right to ignore anything that doesn't make sense is a crucial element of any child's learning—and the first right children are likely to lose when they get to the controlled learning environment of school" (1998). This is a hard-hitting statement to make about schools and education, but it is exactly what happens when we ask children to memorize meaningless procedures with little or no understanding. When a student gives the answer of 86 to the problem $81 - 7$, or borrows to solve the problem $1,000 - 999$, or gets an answer of 1,999 to that problem, we know that child has given up the right to make sense and ignore what doesn't. Test writers take advantage of this situation by creating distracters on multiple-choice tests that play into such misconceptions. (See Figure 7–1.)

Many children who have given up making sense of or questioning their results hastily mark C without giving it a second thought, when A is the correct answer and about 1,500 less! Human beings are wired to search for patterns and make sense of their world. It's important to use this innate wiring in children as a driving force in their acquisition of knowledge.

When we are open to children's thinking and they know our expectations include persistence and making sense of what they do, they can surprise and impress all of us with their ingenious ways to solve problems.

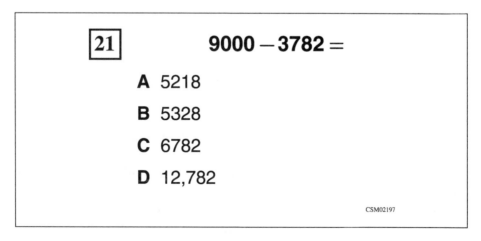

$$\boxed{21} \qquad 9000 - 3782 =$$

A 5218

B 5328

C 6782

D 12,782

CSM02197

FIGURE 7–1   One of California's 2003 Grade 3 released test items.

Sometimes they come up with ways to solve problems that teachers have never thought of; often these surprising ways of thinking reveal deep mathematical understanding and clever connections among ideas, perhaps linking old learning to new situations.

An example of this came from a third-grade student, Tuheen. During a discussion about addition strategies, Tuheen shared the following as a way to solve 36 + 48: "I decided to write the problem vertically. First I wrote ten, then thirty-six, then plus forty-eight." Maryann recorded on the board:

$$
\begin{array}{r}
10 \\
36 \\
+48 \\
\hline
\end{array}
$$

She was a bit taken aback by the ten and asked Tuheen about it. He explained, "Just by looking at the problem, I knew that the six and eight in the ones place would be more than ten. So I showed that by writing ten first. In fact, six plus eight is fourteen. That's four more than ten. I wrote the four under the ones column and then added the tens column. There are eight tens. That's eighty plus the four from the ones column is eighty-four."

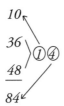

Wow! Such a powerful idea that so clearly indicates sense making and represents what happens when we regroup. Of course this idea can be extended and applied to adding larger numbers or more than two addends. Many of Tuheen's classmates clearly understood his thinking and have since started using it in their own work.

Providing students with interesting and meaningful learning opportunities, along with tools to use to make sense of a situation (manipulatives, 1–100 charts, number lines, ten frames, calculators, paper and pencil, pictures, and so on), followed by written or oral opportunities to show their thinking support sense making and clearly show students its importance.

Students who understand and apply sense making quickly find the solution to test questions such as the following, from the Michigan Educational Assessment Program:

Emma had 80 cherries. She put an equal number into each of five bowls. How many cherries did she put in each bowl?

A. 16

B. 30

C. 88

D. 400

(From Fall 2007 Michigan Educational Assessment Program, grade 6. N.FL.05.05: "Solve applied problems involving multiplication and division of whole numbers.")

A student who makes sense of the problem can immediately eliminate C and D, as both answers are larger than the number of cherries to be put in the five bowls. B is fewer than the eighty cherries to be shared but still makes little sense if eighty cherries are to be put in five groups. That leaves A. Students have only to make sense of the situation and the answer choices to find the correct answer.

The Creation of an Environment That Encourages Risk Taking

A safe and comfortable classroom environment is necessary to nurture within our students the constant desire to make their best effort and to persist until the learning at hand makes sense. Creating a supportive, caring classroom environment from the first moments includes setting forth rules for all. These might be rules you set, or you may ask your students to develop rules, or you could set some rules and ask students to create some. To be effective, rules must

- apply to all students,
- be simple,
- be few in number, and
- ensure safety and respect for all.

Following are two example sets of classroom rules, but you'll need to make choices that work for you and your class:

- Be fair and friendly.
- Work thoughtfully.

- Take care of materials.
- Start work and clean up in a timely manner.

or

- Follow directions.
- Keep hands, feet, objects, and mean thoughts, words, and deeds to yourself.

The important thing about rules is that your students have a chance to discuss them and practice them so that everyone understands them and feels their beneficial effects. Rules make it easier for everyone to work together and for each person to do his or her best work.

Another important way to create a safe classroom environment is to make it clear to students that mistakes are a natural part of learning. From the start, let your students know that in your classroom, mistakes are viewed in a positive rather than negative light. We need to help students realize that errors are prime opportunities for learning. Remind students of Thomas Edison and the thousands of unsuccessful attempts, or mistakes, that had to happen before he found success with the lightbulb. In addition to sharing stories about others, we can model being intrigued rather than embarrassed by our own mistakes. When we make it explicit that an error has led us to rethink an issue and come to a new understanding, we join the community of learners in our classroom, strengthening our ties with our students.

Establishing the belief that mistakes are a part of learning and golden opportunities from which to learn along with implementing respectful rules for all serve as a good foundation for a safe and productive learning environment.

Communication and Discussion

Sharing and listening to ideas gives students the message that you believe they have much to say about mathematics and much to learn from one another. Encourage them to engage in mathematical discussions about a variety of problems and situations, and create a strong expectation that they must listen to each other intently and with respect, even when they disagree with one another. Respect for others' ideas is paramount to creating a culture of safety. We can use our own behavior to model respectful ways of listening, responding, agreeing, and disagreeing.

It's especially important to provide plenty of wait time before accepting answers to questions that we have posed to the class. That way, all children have a chance to think through the question. You can ask students not to put their hands up to answer a question until you've given a signal that the thinking period is over. The first time you make this request, have a discussion about the reasons underlying the procedure. This discussion will help students understand that everyone's thinking is equally valued, that each person has the right to focus on his thinking without being pressured by others, and that people who come to answers quickly need to respect those with different thinking styles.

At the beginning of the year, give students time to purposefully practice restating what a classmate has said during a discussion. The ability to restate what another person has said requires active listening, a habit that is essential in a classroom that uses discussions as an important forum for learning. Model this idea for students by restating what a student has said, always checking with the student to see if you have accurately understood and rephrased her thinking.

Student involvement in discussions should include responding to each other's ideas. Students can be encouraged to state why they agree, disagree, or have questions about what a fellow student has stated. When mistaken ideas are uncovered, it's important to go back to the originator of the mistake and ask if he now wants to modify the original idea as a result of hearing what others had to say. This is an opportunity to reinforce that errors are a natural part of learning and a chance to learn something new. Over time, your students will come to feel comfortable saying, "I'm not sure if this is right, but I was thinking. . . ." An atmosphere in which students are willing to make conjectures helps them become more adept at validating or revising their ideas based on their own mathematical arguments or those shared by others. These opportunities to share and use good mathematical thinking will support students when confronted with a wide variety of test questions. They will have the confidence to make sense of the question and apply what they know to find a correct solution.

One way to establish discussions as an important, ongoing part of learning is to pose true-or-false number sentences to your class. Start with one that everyone is likely to agree on:

- $3 + 1 = 4$ (would be appropriate for young students)
- $1,230 - 101 = 1,129$ (would work for older students)

Explain to the students that you want to know if the sentence is true or false *and* why. After the first person has responded with true or false and his reasoning, follow up by asking, "Did anybody think about it a different way?"

For example, Maryann wrote *True or False? 434 − 110 = 324* on the board at the start of class for a group of fourth graders. She asked the students to quietly consider this problem for a few minutes. After a minute of quiet thought, she signaled that students could raise their hands if they had something to share about the problem. Many hands danced in the air.

Olivia said, "It's true. I know because I counted up from one hundred ten to four hundred thirty-four. I counted one hundred ten to two hundred ten, that's one hundred; then two hundred ten to three hundred ten, that's two hundred; then three hundred ten to four hundred ten, that's three hundred; then four hundred ten to four hundred thirty-four is twenty-four more. So that's three hundred plus twenty-four for a total of three hundred twenty-four."

Maryann asked, "Did anybody think about it a different way?"

Jose explained, "I think it's true, like Olivia said. But I did it differently. I know that four hundred thirty-four minus one hundred is three hundred thirty-four, and then take away ten more and it's three hundered twenty-four."

"Did anybody think about it a different way?" Maryann asked again.

Megan shared, "I think it's true, too, and I did it a way that wasn't too easy. I knew there were eleven tens in one hundred ten, so I counted backward from four hundred thirty-four by tens eleven times. Like this: four thirty-four, four twenty-four, four fourteen, . . ." Megan continued in this way, holding up a finger each time she counted back by ten until she had used all of her fingers plus one more to indicate she had counted back eleven tens. She stopped on 324.

Austin said, "I did it like Olivia, but Jose gave me another idea. He said to start with four hundred thirty-four and take away one hundred and then ten. But you could switch it and start with four hundred thirty-four, take away ten first, which is four hundred twenty-four, then take away the hundred so it would be three hundred twenty-four."

Asking for another way to think about something establishes with students that you understand that there are many ways to think about mathematical ideas and that you value all ideas. A follow-up question to further engage your students in thinking about equality and how to discuss ideas might be

True or false? $4 = 3 + 1$

or

True or false? $1,129 = 1,230 - 101$

Some students will argue that you can't put *the answer* first. As students share their thoughts, listen neutrally and respectfully to them, remembering to ask each person who shares to justify his or her thinking.

The mathematical purpose for asking these types of questions is to help students understand that the equals sign establishes a relationship between numbers and is not just the signal for doing the operation suggested on the left side of the equation to get an answer on the right side. Extend the activity by replacing the equals sign with $<$ and $>$ to further strengthen students' understanding about relational symbols. Providing these experiences throughout the year enables students to understand and solve problems such as the following sample item, from Maryland's 2006 third-grade sample items. Similar items appear on tests from many other states:

> *On the first day of school at Bridge Elementary, 65 third graders arrived on time and 18 third graders arrived late. At Dale Elementary School, 68 students arrived on time and 17 arrived late. Which number sentence represents the relationship between the number of third graders at Bridge Elementary and the number of third graders at Dale Elementary?*
>
> *A. $65 + 18 < 68 + 17$*
>
> *B. $65 + 18 > 68 + 17$*
>
> *C. $65 + 18 < 68 - 17$*
>
> *D. $65 - 18 > 68 - 17$*

The true-or-false questions you pose early in the year have the primary goal of building a classroom culture that includes having students develop the ability to communicate their ideas and justify their thinking. Follow-up number sentences for young students could include the following:

> $4 = 4$
>
> $3 + 1 = 3 + 1$
>
> $3 + 1 = 1 + 3$
>
> $3 + 1 = 2 + 2$
>
> $3 + 1 = 4 - 1$

Eventually, they can move on to these:

> $3 + 1 = \underline{\quad}$
>
> $4 = 3 + \underline{\quad}$
>
> $4 = \underline{\quad}$

Follow-up number sentences for older students could include the following:

> $3 \times 10 = 10 \times 3$
>
> $4 \times 5 > 2 \times 10$

$3 \, R1 = 16 \div 5$

$63 = (6 \times 10) + (3 \times 1)$

$25 \times 2 < 60 - \square$

During these discussions, you may want to remind yourself that you don't need to rush in to provide the so-called right answers yourself. Understanding of conventions about the equals sign builds over time, and your primary goal now is to give students an opportunity to justify their thinking. If students persist, for example, in thinking that $4 = 2 + 2$ is incorrect, keep asking why they think so. We want to help students rethink erroneous positions and become adept at discussing mathematics.

Talking about mathematical ideas and listening to mathematical discussions are two important ways that your students deepen their understanding of mathematics. They can also serve as important ways for you to tune in to what your students are and are not understanding about mathematical ideas so that you can provide the best instruction possible.

Partner Work and Cooperative Grouping

Working in groups rather than individually has a positive effect on student learning, as noted in *Classroom Instruction That Works* (Marzano, Pickering, and Pollock 2001). Research indicates that keeping the groups small—two or three students—is most effective. Also, tasks need to be well structured and appropriate for the group, with not too much to accomplish but enough to give all members of the group a role. You can decide which students to pair or group together, or you can assign groups randomly, for example, by pulling names from a hat or forming groups based on a common trait such as birthday month, favorite color, or pets. Also, it is important to provide students with independent tasks to practice the skills and processes they must master. Cooperative learning, whether students are working in pairs, as trios, or in groups of four, is a flexible classroom structure adaptable to many situations.

When you introduce children to partner work or cooperative grouping, it is important to remind them that the classroom is a safe place. Respect for self and others is expected. It is also expected that students will listen to one another's ideas. Remind students of the rules set forth at the beginning of the year for your class. Also, remind them about how they have learned to share their thinking, to agree, and to disagree during class discussions. Encourage your students to rely on each other and seek your help only when no one in the group is able to solve the question or dilemma. When children come to you for help, sometimes it is useful to ask them what they have done thus far to resolve their issue. This provides insight into their social skills as well as their mathematical thinking, allowing you to guide them immediately with an appropriate question or suggestion.

Mathematical Tools as Learning Supports

In *Comprehending Math,* Arthur Hyde (2006) suggests that by teaching students to ask themselves a few good questions, we can help them become better problem solvers. He teaches students to create a KWC chart to use the information in a problem to answer the following questions:

- K: What do I know for sure?

- W: What do I want to do, figure out, find out? What is the task?

- C: Are there any special conditions or rules I have to watch out for? (22)

The consistent use of a tool similar to this provides a structure that students can use when they aren't sure what to do or how to make sense of a situation or problem. Using this structure increases access, which deepens students' understanding, encourages persistence, and sparks discussion. It's also a useful tool for approaching problems on standardized tests.

Manipulatives are other useful mathematical tools that support learning. Manipulatives in and of themselves do not hold meaning. The student constructs the meaning and, with that meaning, is able to use manipulatives to further understanding. This is a complicated process and does not occur in the same way for all students. Not all students construct the same meaning for the same tool. Another important point to keep in mind is that "meaning developed *for* tools and meaning developed *with* tools both result from actively using tools" (Hiebert et al. 1997).

Manipulatives and other tools that make sense to students should be available to everyone. Different students may use different tools to solve the same problem, or even the same tool to solve different problems. This is fine as long as the chosen tools support and deepen the student's understanding. It is interesting to note that some state tests include questions involving common manipulatives such as base ten blocks, pattern blocks, and fraction bars. If manipulatives are unavailable for use with state tests, as is often the case, it is a good idea to teach students to draw or sketch manipulatives to help them think about, understand, and solve a problem. Following are a few examples of released test items involving manipulatives.

Familiarity with base ten blocks and how they can be used to represent decimals would support students in solving this problem from the grade 5 Michigan test:

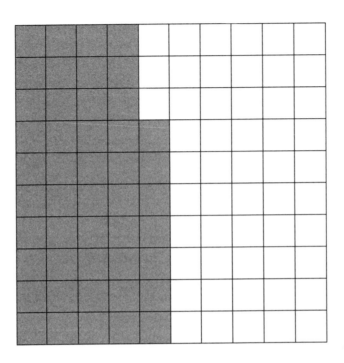

Which best represents the shaded part of the grid?

A. 0.047

B. 0.47

C. 4.70

D. 47.0

(From Fall 2007 Michigan Educational Assessment Program, grade 5.
N.ME.04.15: "Know decimals up to two places and relate to money.")

Experience in making three-dimensional solids with blocks would help students recognize there are hidden blocks in the following example from the Illinois 2007 grade 4 test. Students who knew this would be more likely to figure the correct volume than those who weren't familiar with three-dimensional shapes:

What is the volume of this shape?

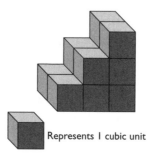

Represents 1 cubic unit

A. *10 cubic units*

B. *11 cubic units*

C. *12 cubic units*

D. *18 cubic units*

Pictures of fraction bars are used on the California 2005 grade 2 test. (See Figure 7–2.) In both examples, experience with manipulatives would increase students' chances of being successful.

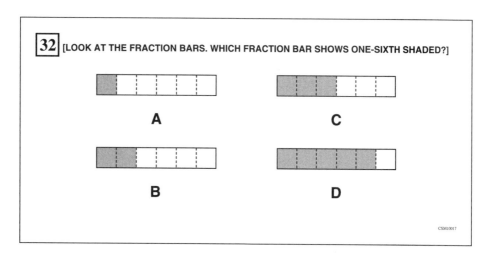

FIGURE 7–2   One of California's 2005 Grade 2 released test items.

Final Note of Encouragement

Not all children are going to come to the same understandings at the same time. If your children are actively engaged in making sense of mathematics, they will grow as learners. By giving your children the chance to think and reason in ways that make sense to them, you also give them the tremendously important message that we each control our own learning and actions. We want our students to become problem solvers who understand and love mathematics. In the face of pressure to raise test scores, it is perilously easy to succumb to reducing math to following procedures without understanding. Resist that urge by developing a supportive classroom environment that encourages children to think, persist, and reason together so they can tackle mathematical problems both on and off the test.

Resources

Following are additional resources that support teaching for understanding:

Carpenter, Thomas, Megan Loef Franke, and Linda Levi. 2003. *Thinking Mathematically: Integrating Arithmetic and Algebra in Elementary School.* Portsmouth, NH: Heinemann.

Chapin, Suzanne H., Catherine O'Connor, and Nancy Canavan Anderson. 2003. *Classroom Discussions: Using Math Talk to Help Students Learn, Grades 1–6.* Sausalito, CA: Math Solutions.

Hiebert, James, Thomas P. Carpenter, Elizabeth Fennema, Karen C. Fuson, Diana Wearne, Hanlie Murray, Alwyn Olivier, and Piet Human. 1997. *Making Sense: Teaching and Learning Mathematics with Understanding.* Portsmouth, NH: Heinemann.

Hyde, Arthur. 2006. *Comprehending Math: Adapting Reading Strategies to Teach Mathematics, Grades K–6.* Portsmouth, NH: Heinemann.

Marzano, Robert J., Debra J. Pickering, and Jane E. Pollock. 2001. *Classroom Instruction That Works: Research-Based Strategies for Increasing Student Achievement.* Alexandria, VA: Association for Supervision and Curriculum Development.

Smith, Frank. 1998. *The Book of Learning and Forgetting.* New York: Teacher's College Press.

Virginia Standards of Learning, Grade 5.

Chapter 8

The Weeks Before and During the Test

As the test date approaches, it helps to think through and schedule time for how you'll help your students deal with the specifics of the test they will be taking. Only you can decide how to do this most effectively. There is no one right answer. Maryann, for instance, prefers to do all of her test preparation within the context of her regular teaching and uses these final weeks to focus on confidence building. Nancy, on the other hand, has the responsibility of getting her students ready for their first ever standardized test and likes to begin introducing the test-prep materials that she's readied for her students right after spring break, about two or three weeks before testing is scheduled to begin. She likes this timing because her students are returning to school rested, after a week free of school demands, and are ready to take on something new.

The amount of directed test practice you choose to do is your call and should depend on your students' past experiences and your own particular testing program. You'll discover what works for you partially through planning and partially through trial and error. You might want to take notes regarding how things go the first year so that you can modify your timing in years to come.

If you have prepared special materials directed toward test preparation, you might find it useful to take a few moments to review them a few weeks before you plan to use them. It helps to think about these materials in the light of what you know about your students' current mathematical development and to make any modifications that make sense. In any case, the goal is to do just enough preparation to make your students ready for the test, but to avoid doing so much preparation that your students are worn down before they begin the test. You don't want them to become careless with their answers because they have become weary of the testing process. When the test itself is a special event, students are more likely to take it seriously and see it as an opportunity to show how much they've learned during the year.

Dealing with Test Anxiety

Most of us probably have a vivid memory related to test anxiety. Here's one that Nancy found very telling from her own classroom experience:

> Some years ago I had the pleasure of taking my class from first to second grade. I remember a moment on the first day of school, as we began our second year together, when Sam announced to the class that this would be the year we would be taking "the test." A murmur of anxiety spread quickly through the room. Several students, like Sam, had older siblings who had described the rigors of standardized testing to their younger sister or brother. I remember feeling somewhat overcome to discover how large testing can loom in children's minds— but I mustered my cool and reminded the class that the test was months away and that by the time it came they would be ready for it.
>
> This incident reminded me that one of my test-preparation jobs would be to ease my students' anxiety. I wanted them to be free of the burden of worrying about the test early in the year so that they could keep their focus on learning. I also made a mental note that as the testing date neared I would need to deal with this anxiety because it is so unfair to place this kind of burden on children and also because it could prevent my students from having access to their best thinking when taking the test.

When it's time to get ready for the test in earnest, it can be very helpful to preface your more focused test-preparation activities with a discussion about the test. Your introduction might include these points:

- The test is primarily intended to let the state know that students are having an opportunity to learn what is important for them in school. It helps students to hear that the test is a way for adults to know if the school's math program is a good match for learning important math concepts. Assure children that they have been learning what's important all year long and that in the next few weeks they'll learn some test-taking procedures that will let them show their learning.

- Explain that doing one's best on the test is the most that any test taker can do.

- Clarify that one can do very well on the test and still mark some questions incorrectly. Explain that the test makers don't want everyone to end up with the same score, so they often include some items that are really meant for older students. Getting those problems correct is not expected of a good student in their grade. You are likely to be able to say honestly (given the ambiguity of some of the items on the reading portion of the test) that even a teacher might not mark every answer exactly the way that the test makers consider correct.

- If it's true, tell your students that test results will not determine if they go on to the next grade. It can help immensely to get this out in the open—you may notice the collective sigh of relief that often follows this announcement. Explain that the test they'll be taking will show some of what they've learned during the year, but that no test can assess all of the many things that they can do as students and therefore should not be used to make decisions about promotion.

- If the test results do determine promotion, another approach is clearly needed. At all cost, it's important to avoid using the test as a threat—a tack that seems very unlikely to foster success. Instead, assure your students that you'll be using the next few weeks in order for them to develop skills to use when taking the test and that their hard work can pay off. Encourage students to air their anxieties about not passing the test, and the consequences, knowing that getting things out in the open can be the first step toward dealing with them.

After making these introductory remarks, it can be useful to encourage your students to ask questions, share concerns, and discuss whatever is on their minds regarding testing. A soothing voice and the goal of inspiring confidence rather than fear in children are likely to be most effective in preparing them to take on the challenges of the test.

Practicing for the Test

Large-group work
Working together as a whole group can be an effective way to help students learn to decipher test language, become more capable at interpreting problems,

gain skill in thinking through answers, and learn how to fill in bubbles. You can use large-group practice sessions to

- look at problems that include understandings that children have been working on all year but are presented in formats that are different than they've seen in the past;

- clarify test language that may be confusing for students to interpret;

- help children settle into solving problems with the support of you and their peers; and

- build confidence and familiarity with the test format.

In the beginning it can be helpful to make the test practice sessions as much like regular classroom times as possible. Pick a type of problem that is likely to be on the test and share it with the class on the overhead or board. In a primary grade, it might look something like this:

$10 + 16 + 32 =$

ⓐ $26 + 32$

ⓑ $36 + 32$

ⓒ 48

ⓓ 42

Students who have never seen a bubble answer sheet can be thrown by this setup. They need an explanation that the lettered options are all the possible answers for the missing information, and they need time to talk about which answer makes sense and why. Give students the opportunity to turn to their math partner and discuss which answer is correct. When the class comes back together again for a group discussion, ask volunteers to explain their thinking. This approach helps students see that test items that may seem confusing at first are just a different way to get at familiar mathematical ideas. It gives children the chance to confront the language and format of the test in a supportive atmosphere and ideally allows them to interpret problems accurately and in such a way that they can access their understanding about the concepts.

On another day a primary teacher might show a problem with the three two-digit addends lined up vertically, a format that isn't normally used in class. With the chance to discuss what the problem is asking them to do, and how they might go about solving it, partners are likely to come up with methods that work for them. It helps to make scratch paper available so that they can use their usual method(s) of determining the answer and get used to doing their work in a place other than the answer sheet.

As before, the class can come back together as a large group to share strategies. These discussions encourage students to solve problems in ways that make sense and are efficient. It can help students feel increasingly confident if they have several opportunities to reiterate how the test's way of presenting a concept may be different in format or language, but is really just asking for something that makes sense and is familiar. The main idea is to empower students, making them feel that the test is not such a big deal after all.

It's hard not to become annoyed at the need to spend time on test preparation—after all, this time could have been spent on introducing a new unit of study. Nevertheless, when approached in this collegial, problem-solving manner, test preparation that reviews previously presented concepts that are arranged in order from easiest to most difficult can actually have another positive outcome: it may help some students solidify and even extend their learning. It's gratifying to see some lightbulbs turning on while test preparation proceeds.

Small-group work

When you feel that your students have become more confident in approaching test problems, bring out the practice sheets that you prepared earlier in the year. It's generally best to start with the easiest. You might even choose to start by working through some of the problems as a group, but eventually you should have your students do the problems individually, with plenty of opportunity to discuss their thinking with a partner. You may want to continue to have times when strategies can be shared and answers discussed with the whole class; at other times you may prefer to have individual conferences with children to either reinforce their thinking or help them deal with problems that have been difficult for them.

Another option, which would work particularly well for older students to continue to use the supportive small-group structure. You may or may not want to assign roles, but the group can perform these four tasks for each problem:

1. Read the problem.

2. Clarify the problem; figure out what it is asking.

3. Solve the problem using one strategy.

4. Solve the problem using another strategy to confirm or to correct the answer.

If you assign roles, make sure the roles rotate frequently so that each group member has practice doing each of the tasks.

The important thing during this stage of test preparation is to avoid a test-taking atmosphere and instead let your students use their usual methods of solving problems in a collegial atmosphere, making it possible for them to become familiar with the test sheet format and confident about their ability to understand and solve test problems. They'll draw on these experiences when you move on to the next stage of test preparation, giving them just a taste of what it's like to work without the support of feedback from classmates and teachers.

Individual practice: Going it alone

You'll also want to give your students a chance to have a few sessions that more closely mimic the test-taking experience. You can use the practice test provided by the test makers, which is intended to get children familiar with the test format, or use other practice sheets that you've prepared or come across. By this time your students will know the bubbling-in procedure and just need some time to practice working entirely alone. You may decide to end these sessions by sharing feelings and discussing how working alone is different from being able to get and give support. You may find that some children like it and others find it daunting. For those challenged and frustrated by the isolation, try to help them remember that although they have to work alone while actually taking the test, they can draw on all those previous conversations with their partners and with the class in order to access strategies that helped them be successful.

If your students will be confronted with a test in which some harder problems appear earlier than easier problems, make sure that students know they should not give up just because they come to a difficult problem. This kind of knowledge can help your students realize the value of trying to answer every problem.

Introducing new units of study

Some of the test-prep materials that you have prepared may require a slightly different practice format, such as those introducing mathematical concepts for the first time. For example, recall the discussion about teaching fractions to second graders in Chapter 2. With this particular unit, you might first do the activities with cubes (described on page 21) to build a foundation for the worksheets. Then the class could go through the entire set of written problems together, one by one. In this way the concept building and the test preparation come together in one neat package that takes little time away from the more developmentally appropriate mathematical work that is central to children's long-term mathematical growth. You'll get the biggest payoff if you do these kinds of units very close to the test-taking date so that the ideas will be fresh in students' minds.

Test-Taking Strategies

Thinking about specific test-taking strategies can be helpful to students, so you might want to take some time to practice some of these strategies with your students as part of getting ready for the test. Only you can gauge which of these strategies might be helpful for your students to practice and which of them match the maturity level of your students. Young children, for instance, might be overwhelmed by trying to learn too many of these techniques, but older students may benefit from some experience with all of them.

Learn when to make a best guess and move on

If the test you administer does not impose a penalty for wrong answers, students of all ages should know that it pays to make a guess even if they are not sure of an answer. It may be especially important to teach this practice to students with a strong tendency to be perfectionists. Students need to practice dealing with that agonizing situation when more than one answer seems correct—or when none of the choices seems good. They need to learn that it doesn't pay to get bogged down by one problem. Discuss how frustrating it feels when one faces this situation, but make it clear that it's OK and even wise to make a best guess when a clear choice does not present itself. Remind your students that if they've been thoughtful in their approach to the problem, they have a very good chance of marking the correct answer. Help your students become comfortable saying, "I think it's best-guess time."

Read the whole problem carefully

Teach your students to read each question carefully. They need to take the time to clarify in their own minds what the question is asking. They also need to practice attending to such details as plus and minus signs in computation problems. Test makers can be purposefully tricky, so it helps for students to have practice with items where one of the answers would be correct if the problem could be solved with addition, but is the wrong answer because it actually involves subtraction.

Eliminate unrealistic answers, or ask, "Does the answer make sense?"

All year long you've been encouraging your students to make estimates to determine if an answer makes sense. This skill is important mathematically and also helps students eliminate unrealistic answers during test taking. You might want to have sessions with your students that emphasize using estimates in test-taking situations. Start with some easy and outlandish examples:

75 + 98

Is the answer more likely to be 12 or 173? How do you know?

1,658 − 5 = □

Is the answer going to be less than a thousand or more than a thousand? How do you know?

Devise other problems that are closer to the ones that your students might encounter on the test to bring home the point that often computation down to the last digit is much less important than examining all the answers and eliminating those that are clearly not possible.

Think inside the box

Sometimes students mark the wrong answer because they are better mathematicians than the test makers. Students might mark the wrong answer for a question like this:

How can you prove that 5 + 4 = 9?

A. 9 − 5 = 4

B. 9 + 4 = 5

C. 9 + 5 = 14

D. 5 + 5 = 10

For instance, they might mark D even though A seems such an obvious correct answer to those of us who are aware that the test makers designed this problem so that students can show they understand the inverse relationship between addition and subtraction. But of course, D is also a way to verify thinking about this type of problem. The students who mark D may understand the inverse relationship of addition and subtraction, but in this instance their minds go to a more direct number relationship: if 5 + 5 = 10, then 5 + 4 has to = 9.

Make sure to discuss this type of problem with your students. Explain that although either answer could be justified mathematically, the test makers designed the question to test their knowledge of how addition and subtraction relate to one another. Make it clear that it is their right to mark whatever answer they want, but if they want to get the problem correct, they have to think like the test makers.

You are likely to find other instances like this one among the test-preparation materials for your grade level. Spend some time discussing the particulars of those problems with your class. You may also want to clue your students in to the notion of thinking inside the box in general when taking a standardized test. Older students especially need to know that one of the major flaws of multiple-choice tests is that they don't allow test takers to justify their reasoning. And they also need to know that they can become adept at outguessing the test makers.

Test each answer that is not unrealistic to see if it works

Once unrealistic answers have been eliminated, it is sometimes efficient to try out each of the other possible choices by inserting them in the problem to see which one works. This can streamline the process of choosing the best answer.

Use the inverse operation to determine which answer is correct

Students can also solve problems by using their knowledge about inverse relationships. For instance, consider this subtraction problem:

$$259$$
$$- 164$$

A. 423

B. 105

C. 95

D. 405

Students can first eliminate A and D because they are unrealistic. Then they can try out the other two answers in addition sentences:

B. $164 + 105 = 269$

C. $164 + 95 = 259$

Bingo! C it is.

Students might do this to check an answer they've already decided is the likely correct answer, or they might do it because they prefer addition over subtraction. The same strategy would work for applying multiplication to a division problem and vice versa.

Administering the Test in a Supportive Environment

As the actual testing period approaches, you may want to spend some time getting yourself and your students mentally and physically prepared for the test-taking periods. Give some thought to discussions and activities that you may want to do with your students. This section outlines some suggestions.

Shifting roles from teacher to monitor

After spending all year making communication a big part of your classroom culture, you will find that during the test you have been thrust into a role that may not feel entirely comfortable. During the test you cannot answer questions or guide your students to new understandings. This shift is major, and if too abrupt, it can affect the culture of your classroom, which you've spent so many months developing. Remind yourself that this change is real and that you need to find ways to mitigate what will be an unusual and possibly uncomfortable relationship with your students.

It helps to talk to your students openly about this situation. Explain that the state wants to have a chance to see what students know about mathematics, based on the problems they will be solving on the test. Remind them that the rules of the test require that each person work independently, but that no one is expected to get every answer correct. Tell them that they may feel uneasy at first and even want to ask for help. Explain that you will be unable to provide it directly, but that they can draw on all experiences they've had throughout the year working thoughtfully, alone and with their classmates. This might also be a good time to talk about how a test can never define a person—it's simply a snapshot of one's thinking on one single day.

Protecting yourself

It's important to be sure that you are familiar with all the protocols of your state's testing program and follow them rigorously. There can be a fine line between preparing children for testing and straying into practices that are prohibited by the rules of the test. It's best to do your own careful reading of state guidelines and not rely on others to have communicated every precaution. It's not unusual to come across a newspaper article alleging some form of cheating on standardized tests by students, teachers, or administrators. The best way to protect yourself from false allegations is to ask that there always be another adult in the room while the test is being administered. Ideally this person will bring the tests to your classroom and then gather them again when the testing period is over and return them to the secure place designated at your school site. A few years ago a former student teacher was investigated by the state because her test scores were so high. She and her students were able to explain that they did so well because of the way she had approached learning all year long, but it was not a pleasant experience for her. At a time when she should have been congratulated for her fine work, she had to defend herself. The process may have been less stressful if she had had another person who could have vouched that she had followed all test protocols.

Controlling the environment
Providing physical comfort
You can't make sure that your students go to bed early and have proper nutrition outside of class during the testing period, but you do have some control over what happens in school. Consider having light snacks available for your students—fruit, graham crackers, anything that is healthy and appealing. Be aware of temperature and air flow in your room to make sure that these kinds of environmental issues support the comfort and well-being of your students.

Suspending homework
Testing is taxing for students. One simple way to take the stress off is to suspend homework during the testing period. This action can be easily justified to parents and administrators as good practice because it can help children be less stressed and therefore more ready to perform their best on testing days.

Relaxing the curriculum during nontesting hours
It can also be helpful to make nontesting class time less arduous on those days when tests are administered. It may make sense to give your students more choice time, and you may even want to consider working on a class project that is fun and collaborative during nontesting hours. One valuable project is making a class quilt. Quilt making doesn't have to be elaborate to help rebuild the sense of community that can be lost as students work in isolation. Anything from a cloth quilt composed of individually hand-sewn geometric blocks to a paper quilt of student drawings around a common theme can serve this purpose. If quilting has no appeal for you, consider introducing another project that brings your students together and lets them use their creativity in a collaborative and purposeful manner.

Providing last-minute review

These days in California, drivers are allowed to renew their driver's licenses by mail if they have a good driving record. But there was a time when individuals regularly had to take the written portion of the test as part of the renewal process. It wasn't unusual to see a long line of people waiting their turn to pick up a copy of the test, their noses in the little booklets provided by the Department of Motor Vehicles (DMV). They were using this wait time to review all the curb markings, speed limits, and distance limits that they would need to memorize in order to pass the test. The line moved slowly so that most people, by the time they got to the head of the line, had enough information stored in memory to pass the test.

You can do the same for your students. In a period shortly before each testing session, go over the concepts that your students may need to brush up on in order to be successful on the test. You obviously can't go over actual test items with your class, but you can do a quick review of the vocabulary and concepts that will be tested, as a kind of warm-up to the test. This process is one that students need to learn to do in order to prepare for important tests throughout their lives, just as drivers do at the DMV.

Preparing yourself

Dealing with your own anxiety

It's hard for a teacher not to feel a fair amount of anxiety during the testing process. These feelings are natural, but not necessarily helpful. Remind yourself that you need to shield your students from your anxiety as much as possible. You can't help your students with the specifics of the test, but your steady presence can have a positive effect on their performance.

The quality of your voice can be important. It's best to use a calm, natural voice when administering the test. If part of the protocol is for you to read test items to your class, think about your own pacing. If a problem involves examining geometric figures or interpreting graphs, for example, let students look at the illustrations for a few moments before reading the problem to them.

It helps to become as familiar with the test as your state protocol allows so that you can present the test with the least confusion possible. If you are unprepared and muddle through directions, your students will pick up on this confusion. Take the time to become familiar with and think through the test directions so that you can introduce the test with as much clarity as possible.

Being a positive presence during the test

Before each testing session begins, remind your students that although you can't talk to them about specific answers, you are there, rooting for them. Smile with warmth and encouragement during the test and deal with issues such as broken pencil points with kindness and reassurance.

Preparing your students

Consider developing relaxation techniques with your class to use before and during the test. These could include deep-breathing exercises, stretching routines, and positive self-talk. Children can learn to remind themselves that they are smart and prepared for the test with a phrase that you choose with your class. "I can do it" repeated a few times with some deep breaths in between works nicely.

A more active routine might include standing and doing *crossovers*. This exercise involves slapping the raised right knee with the left hand and then doing the same with the left knee and right hand. Repeated several times, this activity both dispels pent-up energy and gets the brain waves going. Try it at different speeds for fun and variety.

Maintaining a positive classroom culture

Processing the process

After the first testing period you're likely to feel the need to spend some time as a group discussing how it felt to actually begin taking the test. You might want to preface this discussion with a reminder of the importance of respecting one another's feelings as students share their thoughts. Some students will have found the experience difficult, others will have enjoyed it, and still others may feel the need to swagger as a way of covering up feelings of insecurity that the test created. You can use this discussion to talk about the reality of testing, responding to whatever comes up with as much wisdom as you can muster.

On subsequent days you'll want to take the temperature of your students' moods to see what might be most appropriate. On some days it might make sense to have another discussion, at other times your students may just need to decompress quietly by drawing or reading independently—and there may come a time when you decide to get out the rhythm sticks and let everyone beat on them as loudly as possible!

Celebrating

Consider planning some form of celebration when the testing is complete. You could make a special treat; the strawberry shortcake recipe in the book *Cook-a-Doodle-Do!* (Stevens and Crummel 1999), an updated, cooperative version of *The Little Red Hen*, might be especially appropriate since the recipe itself is delicious, and the message of the book is about working together with kindness. A popcorn party is a more simple and festive alternative. Regardless of how you choose to celebrate, the idea is to mark the completion of a significant experience, validate all the hard work required by the testing, and have fun together. Whoopee—you made it!

Resources

Stevens, Janet, and Susan Stevens Crummel. 1999. *Cook-a-Doodle-Do!* San Diego: Harcourt Brace.

Chapter 9

Communicating with Administrators and Parents

Much of the tension we feel around testing comes from the anxiety that parents and administrators bring to the subject. Their concerns are often fueled by press releases, which tend to overlook many of the realities of the classroom. Combating these misconceptions is not an easy task and we, too, may need to do some positive self-talk in preparation for communicating with parents and administrators. It helps to remind ourselves that we are the true experts and that we know much more about our students than a test score can reveal. It's also true that, although we don't have all of the answers, we do have strong ideas about the kind of support our students need in order to do their best at school.

Communicating with Administrators
About Your Teaching and Test-Preparation Plans

Changing attitudes about curriculum and testing is clearly not an easy task, but it is a way to be proactive rather than reactive. Trying some of the following suggestions might feel more satisfying than getting involved in the downward spiral of negativity that seems inevitably to come about while commiserating with colleagues about tests and test pressures. It's not that this negativity isn't often totally justified, it's just that it tends to lead nowhere. After letting off a little steam, we can use our time together most fruitfully by preparing information and providing support to one another as we get ready to communicate our teaching and test-preparation choices to other decision makers in our districts. With support from one another, we are likely to have better arguments prepared.

We'll also feel buoyed up by the presence of colleagues who can provide ballast to our positions when we present them.

If necessary, begin by finding ways to help your local administrators develop awareness that standardized tests have become more focused on problem solving than straight computation. It can help to share some of the released test items you've gathered to illustrate this point. Such examples help make the point that merely doing pages and pages of computation is not nearly enough to prepare students to be successful on tests. Once you've conveyed this information, you may be ready to explain that your analysis of the state standards and the test suggest the need for a problem-solving program. In contrast to a skill-and-drill program, a problem-solving program will enable you and your students to be better prepared to answer the more complex problems being asked on tests.

You may want to talk about how district pacing guides can be well meant, but are unlikely to result in good teaching for all students. It helps to have your yearlong plan on hand so that you can show how you've thought through the year. You will then have proof that, although you will be basing your daily instruction on assessing your students' understanding, you will not get bogged down and forget to cover all of the strands of math included on the test. You may even want to discuss how you plan to use formative and summative assessments that mesh seamlessly with your teaching to guide you to better prepare your students for the standardized test.

Because the politics of testing is so omnipresent in our society, we often feel that we are taking two steps forward and one step back. But if we don't stand up for good teaching practices and make efforts to inform the public about how our students can best be served in the classroom, who will?

Informing and Reassuring Parents About Your Math Program

Parents may need some of this same help in understanding your approach to teaching. Early in the year you'll want to convey to your students' parents what you plan to do in your math program and why so that they can relax and support your efforts. Throughout the year, continue to communicate with parents about your program so that they develop growing confidence in your approach. As the testing date nears, you may want to give more specific information about the test and testing period. Another one of your goals may be to let parents know that a positive approach to discussing testing with their children is important. Sometimes parents, in their attempts to encourage their children to do well, fall into the trap of pressuring their children unduly and may even threaten their children with being held back a year.

Only you can decide how best to communicate with your parent population about the specifics of your testing program. See if some of the ideas expressed in this sample letter can be useful to you as you craft your own way of telling parents about the specifics of the test your students will be taking:

Dear Room 5 Families,

On Wednesday of next week we will begin standardized testing. Please help us out by making sure that your child comes to school rested and having had a nutritious breakfast each day during the testing period. Expect your child to be tired at the end of the school day and consider cutting back on outside activities during the test period. We are also trying to eliminate as much stress as possible at school. To that end, there will be no homework starting next week and throughout the testing period so that time away from school can be relaxed and free of extra school requirements.

In these past few weeks we've been preparing for the test by doing work that gives your child experience with the multiple-choice, fill-in-the-bubble format of the test. We've done lots of talking with each practice session and so far everyone has a generally upbeat attitude about the test. Some of our talk has been about how it feels to take a test. I made a point to acknowledge that feeling a little nervous is a very natural reaction to taking a test. I've also let the class know that this test will not determine if a student goes on to third grade. When I said this, I could see everyone visibly relax. Such an attitude will make it possible for students to focus on doing their best on the test. Several children were also concerned about getting every answer correct. I've assured them that it's very unlikely that anyone will get a perfect score and that it's possible to miss items on the test and still score very well. This information, too, seemed to diffuse some of the negative tension around testing.

We're doing a lot to make this a positive experience for everyone. Perhaps most important is that all year long we've been encouraging students to think deeply and support their ideas in oral and written form. We think this work has been the best preparation for building test-related knowledge. In these last few weeks, we've emphasized how much students have learned this year and that the test will allow them to show at least some of their growth over the past year.

I also want to remind you that a test score can tell only so much about your child's growth. Multiple-choice tests by their very nature don't allow students to explain why they've made a particular choice. It is possible for a child to mark a wrong answer because he has thought about the problem in a different (and probably more creative!) way than the test makers. That means that test scores need to be read with a grain of salt. There are many kinds of intelligences that cannot be measured by a standardized test and these kinds of intelligences are very important for your child now and in the future. Feel free to contact me if you have any questions when you receive your child's test scores next fall.

I would also appreciate it if you listen for any concerns your child expresses at home regarding testing and do whatever you can to reassure him or her. Please feel free to let me know if anything comes up that I should know about, or if you have any questions about this or any other aspect of testing.

Warmly,
Nancy Litton

Another way to effectively communicate with parents is to get together with your administrator and other teachers to hold a parent workshop. The purpose of the workshop would be to inform parents about the test by sharing released sample test items, explaining how the test is administered, providing guidance about how to interpret results, and explaining that the test is probably not the best way to look at individual students. Help parents to understand how the school uses the results to look at the school's program and how test scores are determined.

Providing Information That Parents Need to Know

Sometimes you'll notice something about a particular student that happened during the testing that you will want to convey to parents and even future teachers. For instance, some children who work carefully and methodically may do an excellent job on the problems that they answer but be unable to complete a timed test. Their slow pace may depress their test scores even though they have strong math ability.

Other children, despite your best efforts, may become so anxious during the testing that they do not do well. You'll want to make sure to convey both your assessment of these students' ability in nontesting situations and also the particulars of what happened during the test. That way parents will have more to go by than a set of numbers that seems to define their children's ability in a negative light.

Resources

Following are some additional resources that support teaching for understanding:

Burns, Marilyn. 1999. *Leading the Way: Principals and Superintendents Look at Math Instruction.* Sausalito, CA: Math Solutions.

Litton, Nancy, 1998. *Getting Your Math Message Out to Parents: A K–6 Resource.* Sausalito, CA: Math Solutions.

Afterword

T *his is only a test*—critical words to remember! Take time to reflect on all that you have done to prepare your students for test success and for future learning. As a result of careful research and decisions, you have provided students with

- a thoughtful, well-planned curriculum grounded in understanding;

- important learning experiences that inspired and developed a sense of wonder and awe, built confidence, and encouraged a love of learning;

- preparation that allowed students to show their academic prowess on standardized tests; and

- a strong foundation that enabled them to move forward, well prepared for future learning.

Tests can tell us where strengths and weaknesses are in our programs, instruction, and students. But few tests, if any, can tell us more than we know already about our children. We work with our students day after day, listening to them, trying to understand their thoughts, ideas, and misconceptions, and guiding them to success. Because we know our state's standards, the types of items on the state tests, and our students, the test results and our perceptions of our students should be closely aligned.

Consider trying the following: Before the testing begins, predict how you think each of your students will do in each of the subject areas tested. Jot down your thoughts. Observe your students as they work through the tests. Look back at your predictions and jot down any changes you'd like to make based on your observations. Do this again at the end of the test. When you receive the results, compare them with your predictions. It is likely that your predictions will closely match how your students actually did. You know your students, and the results of the test should confirm what you already know.

Sometimes, results can be disappointing. The truth is, not all children will perform at the top on a standardized test. It's important to keep in mind that elementary children want to please and will do the very best they can. We must look at each student's scores and growth and consider if they represent the student or not. In many cases, standardized test scores are reflective of the child, but not in all cases. That is when it's important to consider the source of the discrepancy. Consulting the notes we made about our students as we observed them during the testing can reveal causes of discrepancies and perhaps even provide insight into what we could do better next time. It's also important to keep in mind that for a child's scores to remain stable from year to year, the child must make progress in his or her learning. If a child makes no progress, that child's test scores will fall.

Making a silk purse out of a sow's ear

Standardized testing has often led to pressure on teachers and children. It has rarely been a force for good in education. We don't want testing to continue to be such a negative force in so many children's lives. Instead we want students to have the chance to construct mathematical knowledge with enthusiasm and with the willingness to work hard when offered problems to solve and tools to use. We want them to develop persistence and flexibility in their thinking and take pleasure when they have created sense and order out of what was an initially puzzling situation. We hope this book can help you create something positive in your classroom, despite a difficult mandate, and that you and your students can enjoy mathematics together.

Fred Wise, principal at Carrillo Elementary School in the San Marcos Unified School District near San Diego, summed it up well in an email he wrote to Maryann in 2007:

> All we want is for our kids to have the preparation they need to have
> the best possible chance at a great life.

Indeed this is what we all want for our students.

Index